God's Best for You

God's Best for You

Discovering God's Ideal Purpose for Your Life

Marilyn Morgan Helleberg

Macmillan Publishing Company
New York
Collier Macmillan Publishers
London

Macmillan Publishing Company
866 Third Avenue, New York, NY 10022
Collier Macmillan Canada, Inc.

Library of Congress Cataloging-in-Publication Data

Helleberg, Marilyn M.
God's best for you : discovering God's ideal purpose for your life /
Marilyn Morgan Helleberg.
    p.   cm.
ISBN 0-02-550810-5
1. Christian life—1960-   2. Providence and government of God.
I. Title.
BV4501.2.H36953 1988
248.4—dc19   87-33794
                                                                    CIP

Macmillan books are available at special discounts for bulk purchases for sales promotions, premiums, fund-raising, or educational use. For details, contact:

Special Sales Director
Macmillan Publishing Company
866 Third Avenue
New York, NY 10022

First Macmillan Edition 1988

10 9 8 7 6 5 4 3 2 1

Printed in the United States of America

To the One Who said,

"I am the way . . ."

and
to Anita, Beth, Carolmae, Jon, and Verna,
my partners in prayer.

Acknowledgments

Just as a plant requires plowed ground, sunshine, rain, and soil nutrients if it is to grow to matu-
rity, so the idea for this book was nurtured by many
different people. I am very grateful to Terri Castillo,
who prepared the ground and planted the seed from
which the work grew; to Mollie McConnell for her
many hours of weeding and nurturing of the young
plant; and to Mary Ruth Howes for her great care in
providing the final pruning and shaping that brought
the work to fruition. To these and all of the others
who have participated in making *God's Best for You* a
reality, I express my thanks. A special thank you
goes to the members of my family, who have allowed
me space and time, and who have surrounded me
with their love during the hours of writing.

Contents

Invitation

When I was a child, my brother and I often wrote messages to each other with invisible ink (lemon juice), using a toothpick as a pen. When the paper was held up to a light bulb, the "invisible" message would appear.

When God writes personal messages to us, He often does it with a kind of invisible ink in the everyday events of our lives. Until we hold these daily incidents up to His light, we can't read them.

As I've tried to learn more about God's will, I've held many events and circumstances up to His light, and I've been wonderfully rewarded to find that, indeed, personal messages have been written there that were invisible to me before. The discovery of patterns interlinking with other patterns to form divine designs has sometimes startled, often delighted, and always filled me with a fresh sense of wonder at the hidden movements of the Spirit in my life. I have come to know that even with all my doubts and problems and sinfulness, there is a reliable power directing my life, one that is totally beyond the laws of chance or coincidence.

Through these reflections, God has shown me that He is most certainly in control of His universe, and that He is a loving Father who can be trusted to give me His very best. A Bible passage I've heard since childhood has come alive for me in a fresh way. "Which of you fathers, if your son asks for a fish, will give him a snake instead? Or if he asks for an egg will give him a scorpion? If you then, though you are evil, know how to give good gifts to your children, how much more will your Father in heaven give the Holy Spirit to those who ask him!" (Luke 11:11–13, NIV). Since I've learned to think of God's will as *God's best*, the truth of that statement has really entered into my heart. Now I can pray, "Thy will be done," with absolute confidence that what my heavenly Father plans for me really is His best. Once I offer my will to Him, His Holy Spirit, who knows what I need better than I do, lovingly calls forth God's perfect plan for me.

Of course, this doesn't mean that I'll sail through life without problems. It is impossible to reflect on one's life without having to confront a certain amount of pain and brokenness. This book would have been much easier to write if I could have just ignored the negatives—the doubts, fears, insecurities, frustrations, guilts, and all the things that reveal my faults and weaknesses. But it is my prayer that by identifying with my brokenness, you may begin to find the courage to trust God's will to lift you toward your own kind of wholeness.

I hope that in this book you can discover how to find God's direction and purpose for your life, and how to live out His will in your work and your relationships with others. I hope too that you will learn how to find the unique song that God wrote on your heart before you were born. Together we'll discover the unlimited access to God's wisdom and grace that is ours when we unite our will with His, so that there is no such thing as an impossible situation for one who draws wisdom, strength, and courage from God. We'll gain some new tools for making decisions and receiving guidance, as well as fresh perspectives on pain and suffering that will increase our ability to cope. Perhaps, as the invisible patterns of our lives begin to take visible form, we'll notice that they are not separate, but that your pattern and mine are truly linked by the Hand that drew those first bold lines on the dark and formless void and said, "Let there be light."

God has a plan for your life. It is His best for you—today, tomorrow and always.

1

What Is God's Best?

Discover that His will is glorious, not burdensome.

I wasn't ready for my daughter's question. We were walking through greening prairie grass along the edge of the Platte River south of Kearney, where we had camped to watch the annual sandhill crane extravaganza. It was the second week in April and about time for the birds to leave the area for their breeding grounds in the northlands.

Every year in early March, it seems as if the sky opens up and rains birds. Some five hundred thousand cranes spread out over the cornfields of mid–Nebraska, preening themselves, feeding, prancing around in a dance of life that is centuries old yet always fresh and new. For about six weeks they leap and soar and cry at the wind, bringing the grace and the splendor and the pain of poetry into our lives.

Then they're gone again, leaving an emptiness on the prairies and in our lives that's a kind of poetry, too.

Maybe it was the thought of those birds and their invisibly guided journey that made Karen ask, with a thirteen-year-old's trust in absolutes, "How can I find out God's purpose for my life, Mom?"

I searched for an answer as we stood on the river bank, listening to the sound of the flowing waters punctuated by the wild, echoing calls of the cranes. But no solid answer came. For the rest of the afternoon, we continued to watch and listen. Then about 4:30, as the April day began to pull down its shades and the bridge cast long-fingered shadows onto the river, we gathered up our camping gear and walked back to the car. There seemed to be an urgency in the flock now. The playful dance of the birds gave way to a nervous pecking at grain, a noisy chattering, a restless flapping of wings. We sat quietly in the car for a while, watching the drama, knowing that an ancient ritual was about to be enacted.

Suddenly, as if gathered into oneness by some great unseen force, a whole field full of birds lifted into the air. For several moments, the sky was a chaos of flapping wings, straining legs, and stretching necks. Then, in obedience to some internal sense of unity, ragged lines and clusters began to merge. The formation became a single, immense body darkening the sky, circling around and around and around, and finally sweeping across the horizon with measured wing beat, heading northward. A few more minutes and that wide Nebraska sky was clear except for a few pink-tinged clouds . . . and the afterglow of wonder that comes from the incredible grace of seeing with new eyes.

I wasn't able to give Karen a pat answer to her question about the purpose of her life. Perhaps each of us has to answer (and re-answer) that question for ourselves. Yet as we talked quietly throughout the afternoon, I think I was able to pass on to her my solid conviction that God most certainly does have a plan for each life. There was something about the mystery and the splendor of those cranes that seemed to confirm that belief. Watching them was like seeing a parable enacted. It helped us to know that even those events that seem to be random are part of a greater and intensely purposeful wholeness. God's hand, although invisible, is reliable and can be trusted. Just as the cranes find their way, not by trying to control their situation but by flowing with invisible forces, so we can find our way through life by relinquishing each incident, each moment, each relationship . . . everything in our lives to God.

It has taken me a while, however, to come to that view of God's will.

God's Will Is Good News

Have you ever been vaguely frightened by a shadowy figure on your doorstep at night, only to find that it was a friend bringing you a gift? That is a small picture of the change in my attitude toward God's will that has occurred over the years. Many of us, I suspect, grew up thinking of the will of God as something vague and mysterious, maybe even slightly dangerous, not the sort of thing one would freely open the door to, without at least some hesitation. But the good news is that the will of God doesn't have to be a shadowy, mysterious concept. It can be an everyday, active force in our lives. To open ourselves to God's will is to discover a Friend, one who comes bearing gifts—sometimes even gifts we didn't know we needed until they were ours.

Have you ever given up on some problem, fearful that the worst would happen, and then found that the *best* happened instead? I think we sometimes pray "Thy will be done" with a heavy heart, fearful of what that might entail. But once we begin to think of God's will as *God's best,* we can truly let go and trust Him.

Have you ever picked up a box expecting it to be heavy, and found that it was lightweight and easy to carry? God's will is like that. Sometimes we get so sober-spirited when we pray "Thy will be done" that our muscles tense and we mentally gird ourselves to shuffle along under a heavy load. But God's will is not burdensome. It is glorious. It is not a weight to be endured but a promise to be embraced!

In the process of coming to know these truths about God's will, I've prayed and listened my way through many tough questions. Does my life really have purpose? If so, how can I find it? What does it mean, at this very moment, to join my will with God's? How can I really know His best for me today?

Will He help me with my decisions? How? Is suffering part of His plan? Is there a way out of the darkness? Does God *care* about the details of my life, or only the broad outlines? How can my neighbor and I open doors so that God's best can unite our world?

These and other questions are what I want to probe with you in this book, and I hope that the discoveries I have made as I've searched for answers will have meaning for you. Most of all, I hope that our negative views of the will of God will be transformed.

Negative Programming About God's Will

Many of us as children heard the words "It's just God's will" used in a negative way. The things we learned as we were growing up have a profound effect on our beliefs today, whether we're aware of them or not. If we're going to learn to see God's will as God's best for us, it's important to examine our early concepts of what His will means. Some of that old programming may need to be rethought.

When I was in the first grade, on the Thursday afternoon before Easter our teacher told us, "I have a special surprise for every child who gets 100 percent on the spelling test."

As soon as she finished pronouncing the words, I knew that I had a perfect paper. The surprise was a real live baby chick, all soft and yellow and cuddly.

And yes, I could take him home. I think Mother was a little less than thrilled, but we fixed up a box in the basement, with some chicken feed in a Mason jar lid and water in a cereal bowl. I named my new "baby" Chicken Little and carried him around all evening. Once Daddy said, over the top of his paper, "Baby chicks will die if you handle them too much." But Chicken Little was my new love, my doll, my baby. I was his mother and I was taking care of him.

In the morning, I hurried to the warm furnace room and peeked into Chicken Little's box. He was lying on his side, his toothpick legs twitching. I picked him up and ran to Mother. Even as I held him up for her to make my world whole again, Chicken Little's body went limp in my hand and the last glimmer of life slipped out through my fingers.

Daddy's words of the night before seared into me: "Baby chicks will die if you handle them too much." Chicken Little was dead. My soft, yolk-yellow baby was dead . . . and it was my fault!

In her attempt to console me, Mother told me that it wasn't my fault. "It's just the will of God, dear."

I ran out of the house and into the canyon to the east of us, where my brother and I had dug out a "cave" in the side of the hill. I sat there for a long time, thinking about God and His will, and I decided that God must be very mean to will the death of a little baby chicken.

I know that Mother meant well. She was just trying to comfort me. But the words I really needed to hear that Good Friday morning were those of Jesus: "Are not two sparrows sold for a farthing? and one of them shall not fall on the ground without your Father. But the very hairs of your head are all numbered. Fear ye not therefore, ye are of more value than many sparrows" (Matthew 10:29–31). I needed to know that God *cared* about Chicken Little and about me, that He saw my hurt and was there to help me cope with it, that there was even a purpose for Chicken Little's life, as short as it had been.

If we have grown up with such negative ideas about God's will, it's no wonder we have difficulty turning everything over to Him. But God's will is always positive, never negative. Even though we sometimes have to pass through difficult places in our lives, He is there with us and, if we will allow Him, He will lead us through the dark passages into the light. Benedict Groeschel says it so well: "Have I believed that You do not send calamities, but out of them You are able to bring what is better? Have I believed, O God, that Your will is not the good or the better, but the best?"[1]

Unsatisfying Answers

The questions and thoughts that went through my childish mind on that Good Friday morning in the canyon cave were the first of many probings for answers to the unanswerable. All through my growing years, hungry questions nosed their way out of my child-mind like puppies, sniffing, tasting, trying out the world. Of all the repeating questions that have nudged me during the first half-century of my life, I think I've pondered most over the ones concerning God's will. I asked wise people, searched the Scriptures, and prayed about all of these questions, but I seemed to get conflicting answers. I was never satisfied with the explanations I received. The theological arguments I read on the subject only left me more confused.

Then one clear April day, I was in an airplane flying over the Midwest. As I sat there thinking back over my life, once again asking those familiar questions about God's will, I looked out the window. There, some twenty thousand feet below me, stretching both north and south for as far as I could see, was the Missouri River. I'd flown this way before, but I'd never really observed the river. Now I was seeing miles and miles of it, instead of only the small chunks I'd seen from ground level, during visits to Omaha. Yet I still could not see its beginning or end. It stretched on and disappeared over the edges of both horizons.

Suddenly I realized why all the rigid explanations about God's will, all the pat answers, had been so unsatisfying. It was because *God's will is not a static concept but a living, flowing reality*—like a river! My childhood view of God's will had been limited, like my view of the river from the ground had been. What I needed was a whole new way of seeing. I needed to quit trying to pin down God's will and just allow Him to reveal His best for me, incident by incident, day by day, moment by moment. I needed to understand that God's will goes far beyond this moment, this day, even this year; it encompasses far more than my small life span. I needed to see with new eyes.

What does it mean to see with new eyes? It means that I can look back on my life and see it as if for the first time. I can notice the patterns there and see how they fit into the overall design. I can become aware of the hand of God, forming and re-forming me. I can take time to ask myself where I'm going, whether or not it's worthwhile to get there, and what price I'm paying for the trip. I can get quiet enough to pay attention to those gentle nudgings of the Spirit that could move me away from my false self toward my deepest being, my true center, which is my spirit.

In my life there have been times when I have recognized the hand of God acting in ways that often startled and amazed me. But more often than not, the movements of His Spirit have been quiet and subtle, woven almost invisibly into the fabric of my daily experience. Only in looking back am I able to see His stamp on an event and to recognize the unmistakable imprint of a caring Father who lovingly guides His child.

God's Best in My Everyday Life

Even though His will flows out of His own perfection, God does not separate Himself from our imperfections. His will streams right out into the everyday lives of ordinary people like you and me. It's in the ringing of my alarm clock; in the rain on the day I wanted it (and on the day I didn't!); in the flip-flops my mind does about disciplining my son John; in that shiver of guilt I feel about not visiting my mother-in-law more often; in the long, curving rope of life events that changed me from a speech therapist to an English teacher to a writer; in my grief over my father's death and the pain of migraine headaches; in the silly mistakes I've made and the stupid things I've said that have humbled me or adjusted my direction; in those sudden changes of plan that have put me at the right place at the right time; in the frustrations that, once released, brought gifts of new vision. The list goes on. But I hadn't seen these things as the will of God in action until I started looking with new eyes, until I started thinking of God's will as *God's best*.

God's best is active right now, on the earth in the lives of human beings. Wisdom (meaning God's will) speaks, in the book of Proverbs, saying "I was daily his delight, rejoicing always before him; Rejoicing *in the habitable part of his earth; and my delights were with the sons of men*" (Proverbs 8:30–31, italics mine).

This Holy City

God's best is not some unreachable star. It is here. It is now. When Jesus' beloved disciple, John, saw the new Jerusalem, he was not on a space flight. He stood on the Isle of Patmos, right here on planet earth. But he saw with his spiritual eyes. What he saw was not fiction. He saw spiritual truths made visual, an unchanging reality that is actually more real than the one we experience with our senses. He saw a city with streets of gold. The city had twelve gates, and *they were always open.* I believe that those gates into the spiritual city are open, even now. I believe that there can be moments during this lifetime when we step through them and experience, for an instant at least, a reality that is beyond time and space. The point of entry may be a butterfly or a sunset, a symphony or a verse of Scripture. It may be a welling up of praise from within or a cry of the heart that knows its own insufficiency. And suddenly there is the knowing—the deep, sure inner verification of the fact that, although we live in a physical world, we are spiritual beings.

There is a river in the Holy City. "And he showed me a pure river of water of life, clear as crystal, proceeding out of the throne of God and of the Lamb. In the midst of the street of it, and on either side of the river, was there the tree of life. . . ." (Revelation 22:1–2). The tree of life represents spiritual man. Could it be that my spirit is already rooted next to the River of God's Truth? If that's so, then I can, even in this moment, receive life-giving water from it to sustain me during this journey through the wilderness of life. It can be my source of energy on those days when I'm exhausted and I'm sure I can't possibly go on . . . but the strength is there and I do. It can be the quiet reassurance that seeps up through my roots when I have to make a difficult phone call . . . and the right words come. It can be my guide in the loneliness of a heart-wrenching decision. Could it be that the river that flows out of the Holy City reveals to me, piece by piece, God's sealed blueprint for my life?

Yes, I believe it is so. There are many things I'm not sure about in regard to God's purpose, but some things I do know. God truly *wants* to reveal His best to you and me, even more than we desire it. There's something wonderfully comforting in knowing that the force that governs the universe—God's will—has been operating with order and precision since before the world was created. I believe more strongly all the time that ultimately no evil is capable of defeating God. Like the river that flows through the Holy City, God's best is life-giving and creative. Like the gentle rain on my newly planted tomatoes, like the carefully channeled waterflow on Nebraska cornfields, the river that is God's best produces growth, transforms dry, stunted lives into creative lives.

God's will is active and dynamic. I know I can choose to have an attitude of expectancy that God's grace will show itself in my life. This does not assure me of a trouble-free existence, but it creates in me a rock-solid trust that, as long as I stay near Him, I will not drift too far off course, will not be pulled under, will not run aground. God's will can be trusted.

Mapping the River's Course

Whenever I begin a new project, I think about something my Aunt Alta taught me, years ago, about learning new truths. My aunt was a third grade teacher, and one Christmas when I was about eight years old, she gave me a copy of Anna Sewell's *Black Beauty*, which I promptly laid aside in favor of the toys under the tree. But later, after the wind-up doll had broken and the batteries on the laughing tiger had run down, I opened the book and looked at the pictures. Then I turned back to page one, ready to start reading. What a disappointment! The book was much too advanced for me. I can still remember sitting there on the floor, whining, "I don't know this word. I don't know that word," and then with a frustrated "I can't read this!" tossing the book aside again.

Aunt Alta went over and picked up the book and then sat down, cross-legged, on the floor beside me. "If you worry about what you don't know, you'll never learn anything. Start with what you do know, and the rest will come." Aunt Alta put her arm around me and together we started in. I read all the words I recognized, and Aunt Alta filled in the ones I didn't know. She stayed two weeks with us, and during that time, we read all of *Black Beauty*. In the process, I'm sure that my reading vocabulary grew like dandelions in the spring. Aunt Alta's advice still helps me when I'm trying to understand something new. "Start with what you do know and the rest will come."

Even though there are many things I do not understand about God's will, there are certain things that I *know* are part of His plan for my life. Some of them are obvious. He wants me to . . .

- love Him enough to put Him first in my life;
- keep human love in my life, too;

- abide by His moral laws;
- tell others about Him (gently, never trying to force my beliefs on them, remembering that example is the best teacher);
- be a servant, first to Him and then to others whom He gives me to serve;
- recognize my dependence upon Him;
- have a deep reverence for the Bible;
- honor His sacrifice by coming to His communion table.

Some things He wills are not so obvious. He wills . . .

- that there be challenges and growth (and therefore some pain and suffering) in my life;
- that my scars and wounds be healed, that I discover overcoming;
- that I offer Jesus my pain and failures, uniting them to His suffering;
- that I not shut off my feelings;
- that I spend time with Him every day (not so that I may get the things I want, but so that I may come to know Him better and love Him more);
- that I live creatively, aware of His presence within me;
- that I be free, in the sense of Galatians 5:1 ("Stand fast therefore in the liberty wherewith Christ hath made us free");
- that I be true to myself—the self He gave me;
- that I have work to do I find satisfying;
- that I ask for His help with my decisions;
- that I keep searching for answers to the unanswerable, for as long as I live;

- that I make room in my thinking for apparent in-consistencies, knowing that they may lead me to higher truths;
- that I can pray, "Thy will be done," without a sense of resignation to the worst.

In return for seeking His best God offers me some gifts:

. . . increased confidence that life is ultimately meaningful, that He really is in control;

. . . new perspectives on pain and suffering, result-ing in a growing ability to cope;

. . . new tools for making decisions and receiving His guidance;

. . . a remedy for the disease of emptiness;

. . . the discovery that the Holy Spirit is a flowing Stream within me, who understands who I am and what I need and knows how to move me toward realization of my God-given potential;

. . . an eagle-winged awareness that *all* experiences have meaning;

. . . the awareness that there is no such thing as an impossible situation for one who draws wisdom, strength, and courage from God;

. . . the solid conviction that God's will is not bur-densome but glorious, not a restrictor but an enabler, not a stagnant pond but a flowing River.*

---

*The Appendix on pages 239–42 gives Scripture references for each of the preceding statements about God's will and His gifts.

God's Best in Your Choices

Make decisions more easily by trusting God's plan and living His leadings.

Did your teacher ever leave the room while the class was taking a test? I have a vivid memory of that happening. It was in Latin class at McCook High School. Most of us (including me) had been sloughing off on studying our daily vocabulary lists, so Miss Carter had staged a surprise quiz. I remember sitting there all tensed up, knowing that I'd get a zero for the day and that would ruin my good average. Then the principal came to the door and told Miss Carter that she was wanted on the phone. As soon as she was safely out of earshot, pandemonium broke loose. Some students sneaked a look at their books.

Others whispered answers to their neighbors. The room was abuzz. By the time Miss Carter came back, I had all the right answers on my paper. So did everybody else.

The next day, instead of handing back our papers, Miss Carter tore them up in front of the class and marked a zero after each name in her grade book. For a week, we all had to sit in her room after school with our heads down on our desks. We had made a wrong choice. The cost: part of our freedom.

One way you can tell whether or not you're acting according to God's will is this: If you're in tune with His will, your choices will lead to greater inner freedom. Choices made against His will always lead to loss of freedom, both inner and outer.

What is *inner freedom?* If I had chosen not to cheat that day, I probably would have failed the Latin test, but at least I'd have failed it honestly instead of getting my zero dishonorably. I'd have been free from the need to cover up my dishonesty. I'd have been free from the fear that I'd be caught, free from the needling of my own conscience.

Patterns, Forms, Blueprints

How does our freedom relate to God's overall plan for all of us?

My husband is an architect, so for over thirty years I've watched schools, churches, nursing homes, hospitals, and other buildings take form, from an invisible idea in a creative mind to the solid physical reality of an occupied building. Each structure is different because it's planned according to the needs of the people who will be using it. A building is always designed with a specific purpose in mind.

I think that something very similar happens when the Creator of the universe plans a life. In the spiritual realm we have a Master Architect, who has designed a plan for each life. He chose us in Christ, "before the foundation of the world, that we should be holy and without blame before him in love" (Ephesians 1:4). Even though plans created by human minds can never be perfect, God's plan is. It can never, never be destroyed. It will eventually be brought into reality here on earth.

But if God has designed my life, why am I so flawed? If He has a plan for the universe, then why are there such man-made horrors as H-bombs, terrorism, and child abuse?

I have gone with Rex as he inspects buildings under construction, and often the scene seems to be nothing but chaos. Recently, we walked through a church that's under construction in a nearby town. There were waste materials scattered all over the place, the electrician and the plumber were having a yelling fight, sawdust covered everything, the walls were bare and the windows glassless. You'd never have guessed, from the look of things, that out of such a scattered mess would come a thing of beauty. But I have seen it happen enough times so that now I have the utmost faith, even as I stumble over piles of ceiling tile or duck under dangling wires, that the time will come when that church will rise up out of the earth, point its steeple toward the sky, and swell with organ music. There will be a thing of beauty that was not there before. From the drawings on the drafting table, the completed structure will take form, and the two will match. You see, I know the architect and I've learned to trust his ability not only to design a beautiful and functional building, but also to direct the construction process.

I also have the utmost confidence that the Architect of the universe knows what He is doing. His blueprint for the earth is given in Ephesians 1:9–10, (NIV, italics added):

> He made known to us the mystery of his will
> according to his good pleasure which he purposed
> in Christ, to be put into effect when the times will
> have reached their fulfillment—to bring *all things* in
> heaven and on earth together under one head, even
> Christ.

When that comes to pass, the blueprints God has already created in the realm of spirit will match the conditions of the physical universe.

The Mess I've Made

Just as we in our Latin class misused our freedom, so it is possible to use our free will, to mess up God's plan for the world and for our lives.

In my husband's business things often go wrong

with the buildings he designs. The manufacturer sends the wrong doors, or the contractor misreads the plans and places a partition two feet to the left of where it's supposed to be, or the brick masons are careless and a wall is not quite plumb. But the significant fact here is that all of those mistakes affect only the physical form. The original *plan* is untouched by them and can be reinstated at any time. Nothing of its perfection is ever lost! It's the same with the blueprints God has drawn for your life and mine.

One thing I've noticed is that when all of the different workers on one of Rex's buildings make it a point to keep referring to the plans and specifications, which are always open and in use at the building site, the construction process goes smoothly and there are few serious problems. If they don't understand something, they ask my husband to explain it.

I believe the same kind of relationship exists between the Architect of the universe and those of us who are trying to build our lives according to His will. If we keep referring to the plans and specifications He's put down for us in the Bible, and if we bring all of our questions to Him, *He will guide the construction. He will make sure that the finished building matches His plan.* Just knowing that is a tremendous relief. *I* don't have to do it all. I don't have to perfect myself. If I stay in close touch with Him, in spite of my sinfulness and terrible mistakes, *He* will keep adjusting my course to His invisible dimensions.

That may require some tearing down and starting over. I once stood with Rex as he called to brick masons on scaffolding some twenty feet above the ground and told them to tear down a wall because it wasn't perfectly straight. You can imagine the moaning and groaning and complaining *that* caused. But the day the building was dedicated, one after another, the bricklayers shook my husband's hand and thanked him for demanding from them the best they had to give.

In an article I read recently, a teacher who worked with high school drop-outs told about her philosophy. Her first statement to every class was always "No matter how many times you've failed in the past, you *will* succeed in this class. *I will not let any of you fail.*"[1]

God is that kind of teacher! "The steps of good men are directed by the Lord. He delights in each step they take. If they fall, it isn't fatal, for the Lord holds them with his hand" (Psalm 37:23, 24 TLB).

There is something tremendously strengthening in the realization that, even at this moment, as messed up as my life is in so many ways, God's perfect plan for me is still there, undamaged by my bumbling. His best for me is the same today, tomorrow, and always, and I can reconnect with it at any moment. My life can never get in such terrible shape that the Architect gives up on me. Of course, that doesn't give me the license to go on making the same mistakes. It just means that He is overseeing the whole process and will take control, *if I allow Him to.*

So yes, I do have free will, but if I ask my Creator to guide that freedom, He will do it. God's best for me requires nothing less than the gift of my will, *in return for which He will give me His!*

The Pattern is Already There

If I insist upon my will and my way, I may think I'm exercising my freedom. But am I, really?

Lucille was an attractive woman in her forties who told me her story at a weekend retreat in Omaha. For years, her husband had carried on one extramarital affair after another. He was also an alcoholic who refused to get help for his drinking problem. But Lucille was determined to keep the family together for the sake of the children. For seventeen years, she expended all of her energy on trying to make that pattern work. Every night she prayed for God to change her husband. Every night she brought her problems and those of her family before the Lord and told Him exactly what He should do to straighten things out. Then one night, her fifteen-year-old son took a potentially lethal dose of sleeping pills. Lucille found him on the floor of his room and was unable to wake him. They rushed him to the hospital. Fortunately they got there in time to save the boy's life.

In the family counseling sessions that followed, Lucille discovered that she had been trying to impose an arbitrary pattern upon herself and everyone else in her family. "I thought it was up to me to make the pattern work," she said, "but there were so many pieces and it was so hard to see where they all fit. Sometimes they wouldn't go where I tried to place them, and the more out-of-place pieces there were, the harder it became to hold the pattern together."

When her son tried to take his life, Lucille just gave up. She couldn't hold her pattern together anymore, so she simply quit trying and told God, "If you want this family to stay together, You're going to have to do whatever needs to be done, because I'm just going to let it fall apart. I'm too tired to be in control anymore."

Then a most amazing thing happened. "I was suddenly aware," she said, "that all that time I'd been holding up nothing. Absolutely nothing. All the weight was on Christ . . . and it always had been!"

Gradually, the jumbled pieces started finding their natural places. Free from her self-imposed burden, Lucille followed up on a long-held desire to take an art class. She also began spending three mornings a week reading to blind children at a nearby school for the handicapped. Instead of losing her freedom, she began to find her true self. Relieved of pressuring from Lucille, her husband began to attend AA meetings. Her children, freed from her well-meaning but stifling domination, started to blossom. It didn't happen overnight. But it did happen, once Lucille let go her control and surrendered to God.

"I found out that it was not up to me to make the pattern," Lucille told me. "God's pattern was there all along. My job was only to discover it, to find the underlying order that was *already there.* In doing that, I found myself."

As with Lucille, sometimes the most effective choice you and I can make is the choice to get ourselves out of the way so that God can put His plan into effect.

His Will Within Me

Where should I look for God's will? Where can it be found? It is always at home within me. *He has planted it in my heart.* "The word is near you; it is in your mouth and in your heart" (Romans 10:8 NIV). That doesn't mean that I shouldn't seek advice from others, or look outside of myself for answers to my problems and questions. What it does mean is that if I offer my will to God every day and ask for His guidance in my choices, when the right answer presents itself, there will be something within my soul that will respond to it. It's that "still small voice" of 1 Kings 19:12. The direction may come through my Bible reading, or by the wise counsel of a friend, or through trying out alternatives, or in some other way, but the *validation* comes from within. There's nothing mysterious about this. I'm sure you've experienced it when, after the first few notes of a song, you think, *I know that tune. What is it?* A few more notes go by as your mind sorts through its patterns. Is it this song? Is it that one? Suddenly a title comes to mind and you know immediately it's the right one. The musical pattern for that song was already imprinted within you. It was there even when you couldn't think of the title. But once the notes you were hearing matched the pattern your mind had called up, there was no longer any doubt.

God has given you the gift of free will. You can use it to get in tune with His will. As this begins to happen in your life, you will become aware of a living pattern unfolding within you, like a rose opening itself, petal by velvety petal. A realm of exquisite order, intelligence, and creative potential will begin to reveal itself. Oh yes, there will be winter times, too, when the rose seems to disappear or die. Yet even then, God's will smiles within you, waiting only for spring.

As surely as the unfolding rose is in the planted seed, God's will is planted within you. It is an active, living thing, waiting only for your recognition. Even if you think you don't have enough faith, *will to believe it* and your unchained spirit, riding on the wind, will convince your mind. Trust God's will to unfold from within you, and His best will surely come to you.

Who's in Control Here?

If God's will is to unfold from within me, I need to make one decision before all others. I must decide to subordinate my will to that of my heavenly Father. It's the only way my life can have unity. Without that unity, I'll become fragmented and my daily decisions will pull me apart at the center.

But listening to God is not as easy as listening to an earthly father, who is physically present and who speaks in a loud voice. Our heavenly Father is invisible and He speaks in a very small, quiet voice. How can I know what His will is in a specific decision?

There are some very concrete things that you and I can do to help ourselves tune in to God's will, so that our decisions will become easier. One of these is to increase the amount of time we spend listening. I can't expect God to make Himself heard to me if I listen only when I have a tough decision to make and want His guidance.

When our kids were little, I went to a meeting one evening and the babysitter put them to bed. When I got home, I peeked in and found little John still awake, so I said, "Did you say your prayers?"

"No," he answered, "but that's okay. I don't want anything from God tonight."

All of us, I suspect, occasionally fall into that trap of coming to God only when we want something (whether it's guidance or something more tangible), and sloughing off at other times. But I keep trying to remind myself that prayer should never be an effort to persuade God to do *my* will, but an effort to lift me to the point where I can know *His* will. *One of the most important purposes of daily prayer is to tune us in so that we can know what to pray for!*

Ask for an Assignment

There is a very simple routine that you can make a part of your daily prayer time. (I'll say more about daily prayer in a later chapter.) It will help to keep you tuned in to God's will, so that when you need guidance on specific decisions, you'll be able to hear it. This is the way it goes:

> Start each morning by asking the Lord for an assignment.
> Stay in prayer until He gives you one.
> Then carry it out.

That's all, but this simple routine will give you priceless practice in listening for the Lord's guidance. "He calls his own sheep by name and leads them out. When he has brought out all his own, he goes ahead of them, and his sheep follow him because they know his voice" (John 10: 3–4 NIV).

At first you'll probably wonder whether it's His voice or your own, but as long as the assignment won't interfere with anyone else's good, go ahead and carry it out. The more you listen for His voice, the easier it becomes to recognize when you have a big decision to make. This kind of "daily assignment" prayer keeps you tuned in.

Here's an analogy that may focus this idea for you. There's only one radio station in our area that I ever listen to, so I keep the dial set at that frequency, even when the radio is turned off. Then, when I want to hear some good music or listen to a special program, all I have to do is to turn on my radio. No fiddling with the dial, trying to locate what I'm waiting to hear. Listening for a daily assignment from God keeps you tuned to His station, even when you're not consciously praying. Then, when decisions come up, all you have to do is turn to Him in prayer and you will begin to hear His voice. (Even though I use the word *voice,* most people do not literally experience divine guidance as a voice. It may come in words, images, feelings, or even in being led to some external source such as a book, a friend, or a teacher who will tell you just what you need to know.)

I know that this type of prayer does tune me in, because sometimes I'm regular about it and sometimes I'm not, and the contrast is really quite striking. When I neglect this "daily assignment" prayer, my decisions begin to get tougher. I have trouble determining what the Lord wants me to do. But when I'm faithfully practicing it, the guidance I receive is often surprising, direct, and right on the mark.

The assignments He gives me are usually little, everyday sorts of things: Call Mrs. Raasch (a shut-in); write a letter to Janelle (a woman who lives in California and who gets depressed); fix corned beef for Rex tonight (a favorite that makes him feel loved). Sometimes God's directions are tougher: Forgive E. and let her know it; offer to help with the upcoming Cursillo weekend; examine your conscience to see what's getting in the way of your relationship with Me.

As you begin to pray this way regularly, you'll find some rather surprising things happening. In the examples given above, Mrs. Raasch told me about a book that helped me a lot with an article I was writing at the time. Janelle wrote back to say that she'd been feeling "down" when my letter came. On the day of my assignment to fix corned beef, Rex came home with his self-esteem stinging from an incident at work. Of course, you won't see such direct connections every time. You may never know exactly why you were given a particular assignment. But know this: At the very core of your being, the Holy Spirit dwells, *knowing*. If you will be a flute through which His whisperings may flow out into action, your life may become a song.

Try to get into the habit of asking for a daily assignment and carrying it out. The more obedient you are to His gentle nudgings, the more *direct* they will become!

A Model for Our Decisions

Even though the specific circumstances of Jesus' life are different from mine, I've come to believe that *there is a model in His life for every decision I have to make.* Very often, the question, "What would Jesus do?" plows right through acres of fuzziness, to provide a clear-cut, focused answer. If I'm not sure what He'd do, I can read through the Gospels until I find an incident that applies.

For example, a few years ago I had a long distance call from a young man who told me his problems and then asked me to pray for spiritual healing for him. I prayed with him and we talked for over an hour. A few nights later, he called me again. Eventually, he was calling me two or three times a week and talking for an hour or two each time. (The phone company must have loved him!) I really wanted to help him, but despite all our long hours of talking and praying, the young man didn't seem to be getting any better. Whenever I'd suggest that we cut down on the phone calls, he'd say, "Oh, I couldn't stand that. I *need* your prayers!" The more we talked and prayed together, the more dependent on me he became. I could see that I was not really helping him, and my family was beginning to resent the intrusions on my time. What could I do? I had grown quite fond of him, and I didn't want to hurt his feelings. I was really torn. I began to ask myself that piercing question, "What would Jesus do?" My first reaction was that He would continue trying to help this young man, no matter how draining it was on Him and those He loved. That *would* be the loving thing to do. Or would it?

A friend who knew about the problem suggested that I read John 5:3–9, which describes an incident by the pool of Bethesda in Jerusalem. There Jesus met a man, sick for thirty-eight years, who was waiting for someone to put him into the water so he could be healed. "Do you want to get well?" Jesus asked him. What a strange question! I thought about that a long time. Could it be that there are some people who *don't want* to be healed? Jesus did not put the man in the pool. Instead, He said, "Get up! Pick up your mat and walk" (verses 6, 8 NIV). If our Lord had not challenged him to get up, that man might have lain there the rest of his life, waiting for someone to put him in the pool.

It seemed clear to me then. The next time the young man called, I told him about the insights I'd had after thinking about the story of the man by the pool. "I can't put you in the pool, my friend. If you really want spiritual healing, you're going to have to go directly to Jesus." I taught him a visualization prayer that he could use to invite Jesus to work His miracles of inner healing within him. I also gave him the name of a Christian psychotherapist in his city. Then I told him I'd continue to pray for him but that our phone conversations would have to stop. It was a matter of choice, and sometimes that means saying no when it would be easier to say yes.

I don't know whether or not the young man used the prayer or contacted the therapist. I still feel a certain heaviness in my heart when I think about him. It was a tough choice, but I do not believe that Jesus, if faced with my decision, would have allowed the young man to become increasingly helpless. I believe He would have challenged him. I still pray for my long-distance friend.

A Question of Values

Asking what Jesus would do is very helpful, but that isn't the only element to consider in our choices. Each of us is unique both in ourselves and in the way we follow Christ. I've found that my decisions are so much easier to make when I'm clear about exactly what's most important to me. Here I'm not talking about what's right or wrong, but of *setting up a way to measure future decisions, by determining what matters most to me.* I'd suggest making a list of the things you value most, and then ranking them in the order of their importance to you. *Then* (and this is the kicker), after you've done that, get out your calendar and your check book and see what you spend the most time and money on. What I really value will show up in how I spend those two valuable currencies. When my values list doesn't match my spending of money and time, either I need to be more honest with myself about what's important to me, or I need to consult my values list more often when I'm making decisions. The voice of the prophet calls to me across the centuries, "Why do you spend money for that which is not bread?/and your labor for that which does not satisfy?" (Isaiah 55:2 RSV).

Values, once determined, need to be reassessed periodically. It wasn't until Rex and I had sorted out what was really important to us for the second half of our lives that we were able to make a life-changing decision a few years ago. At that time, my husband's architectural business had been going downhill for quite a while. Even though Rex is a fine architect, the depressed agricultural economy in Nebraska, plus the introduction of metal buildings onto the scene, had slowed area building to a crawl. It had come to the point where the only way to keep the business going was to cash in our savings and/or borrow money. In fact, we had been doing both, for many months.

But the idea of closing the business his father had started sixty years ago was naturally very painful to Rex. Besides, what would he do? He was too young to retire, and we needed an income. There were also people within the family who were pressuring him not to give up the family business. Poor guy. It was such an agonizing decision that he started having cluster headaches that were so bad he'd actually scream in pain, night after night.

I kept praying for guidance for Rex but it didn't seem to come. Then I was given a writing assignment that had to be completed in a very short time, so I went to our Colorado cabin by myself to work on it. While I was there, I began to let go of the tension about Rex's decision. Every morning, I offered it to God in prayer and then released it. Two days before I was due to come home, Rex called and said that he'd been offered a job at the Youth Development Center in Kearney (a state correctional institution for boys). If he accepted it, he'd be Superintendent of Maintenance. In some ways, it seemed to be an answer to our prayers, but for a man who had been a professional all his life, with his own business, it seemed quite a comedown.

When I got home, Rex and I sat down to sort out what we felt was important to us. I'll admit that over the years, it had given my ego a boost to say, "My husband is an architect." But sitting there at the kitchen counter that June day, we both agreed that prestige was not that important to us anymore. So what *was* important? We decided to make a list of the values that really did matter to us at this point in our lives.

I got out paper and pen and wrote "Spiritual well-being" as number one on the list. "Next comes health," said Rex. Then we added: mental and emotional well-being; financial security, enough to be simply comfortable; some time for building our own togetherness and enjoying our children, grandchildren, and friends. Of course, we each had some separate goals, too, but these were the things that were most important to us as a couple.

Once we had something by which to prayerfully measure our alternatives, we could see that, particularly in the areas of health, mental and emotional well-being, and time, the state position had much more to offer. Actually, there wasn't a single category of our "important values" list that wouldn't be met if Rex accepted the new position. That left one question. What about those family members who were making Rex feel guilty about closing the business? We had to decide which was more important to us—the opinions of others, or our own assessment of the situation.

Rex chose to take the state job. It's been a good choice, because it was based on a reassessment of values and the quiet, gentle leadings of the Holy Spirit. God's best for us meant making changes in our own lives for tomorrow.

Expect the Holy Spirit to Lead You

The Thursday afternoon prayer group I meet with intercedes for many people with all kinds of needs.

The categories include such things as physical, emotional, and spiritual healing, job situations, and safe travel, among others. Sometimes, as one of us is praying aloud for an individual on the prayer list, we'll be suddenly moved to pray for a need we didn't know that person had. Often, we've later discovered that the person did, in fact, need that kind of prayer. This happened recently to Carolmae, and she was so startled that she stopped right in the middle of her prayer and exclaimed, "I don't know what made me say that!"

I think this happens because the Holy Spirit *prays in us.* Paul wrote, "We do not know how to pray as we ought, but the Spirit himself intercedes for us." When you don't know what God's will is in a particular decision, ask the Holy Spirit to intercede for you. "The Spirit intercedes for the saints [that's you and me!] *according to the will of God"* (Romans 8:26, 27 RSV, italics mine).

Once you've asked the Holy Spirit to intercede for you and bring God's will to bear in your life, *expect Him to do it.* One of the things that has taken me a long time to realize, and that I'm still learning, is that *the guidance I receive by inner listening is more trustworthy than that which comes by way of my intellect.* This is not to say that I go around making mindless choices. I believe that the best decisions involve a rhythmic interaction between the conscious mind, the inner mind, and the gracing mind of God. But after I've prayed about a decision and mentally weighed the alternatives, if my head tells me one thing and my spirit another, I have pre-decided to follow my spirit.

A question that I've found helpful to ask myself

is "How do I feel about it when I'm most at peace, when I'm quiet and at prayer, with my emotions and my mental activity stilled?" If there's a deep inner certainty at those times, and doubts arise only when I'm pondering the question outside of prayer, I've found that choosing the former alternative is best. Though I have sometimes felt foolish at the time, I have rarely ever regretted a decision made this way. I am learning, at long last, that I can trust that inner Voice, and that it is wiser than my intellect.

For example, several years ago I had a strong desire to give up my college teaching position and become a full-time writer. It was not a very logical thing to do. It would mean less money coming in, at a time when my husband's business was dwindling. It would mean a great deal of uncertainty. I had no assurance that I could publish more than an occasional article or poem. My mind kept busy feeding me all kinds of solid, rational reasons why I shouldn't give up my job. But every night, when I'd go to my prayer chair, close my eyes, and let go of all that internal reasoning, a very quiet, very gentle heart-knowing would begin to assert itself within me. I have never regretted my decision to become a full-time writer.

But Whose Voice?

How can I be sure, however, that the guidance I receive is really from God? Could it be just my own biased thinking—or worse, the voice of the tempter? It's a valid question. The answer is that I *can't* always know for sure. But I have learned, from my own trial-and-error bumblings, to recognize certain tell-tale clues.

Of course, the most obvious eliminator of bad decisions is that the Holy Spirit will never direct me to do anything that would interfere with the good of another person or anything that is not in accordance with the highest standards of right and truth and justice. If at any time I have a prompting of this kind, I should know right away that it is not a leading of the Holy Spirit.

But there are also more subtle ways in which I can be led to make a wrong turn. Jesus' temptations in the wilderness recorded in Matthew 4:1–11 provide some excellent criteria for determining whose voice I'm hearing.

Jesus' first temptation was to turn stones into bread. He answered it by quoting Scripture: "Man does not live on bread alone, but on every word that comes from the mouth of God" (verse 4 NIV). This is a reminder to me that God is more concerned with spiritual success than with material success. Some people have a gift for making money, and there's certainly nothing wrong with that, as long as their motives are right. Greed and acquisitiveness are wrong, whether one is making five thousand or five hundred thousand dollars a year. If making money is not my gift, however, and I think I've received guidance from the Holy Spirit on how I can make a million dollars, I can be pretty sure it's not God's voice I've heard. I need to examine my choices in the light of Jesus' direction to "seek . . .

first the kingdom of God, and his righteousness; and all these things shall be added unto you" (Matthew 6:33). If my choice places undue emphasis on material things, then it's not likely to be a leading from the Holy Spirit.

Jesus' second temptation was to jump off a high place to make God prove that His angels would save Him. Jesus answered, "Do not put the Lord your God to the test" (Matthew 4:7 NIV—another quotation from Scripture). To me, this means that God is very unlikely to tell me to do something foolhardy that places me in great danger, and expect Him to bail me out. Although He might lead me to risk my life in order to save someone who is drowning, He's not likely to advise me to plunge in if I don't know how to swim.

Finally, Satan offered Jesus all the kingdoms of the world if He'd just fall down and worship him. Jesus' reply, "Worship the Lord your God, and serve him only" (verse 10 NIV), was a quotation from Deuteronomy. For me, this is the real slicer. Whenever I'm making a difficult decision, I've found that asking the question, "Will this alternative cause something else (such as achievement, influence, or pleasure) to usurp the place of Christ in my life?" proves very enlightening. If the answer is yes, then I know for sure that it's not a directive from the Holy Spirit.

A good friend and spiritual adviser taught me another way to test my decisions. If I can invite Jesus to participate in the action with me, if I can ask for His help in carrying it out, then it's probably an acceptable alternative.

Plus-Plus and Minus-Minus

Still, there are always those murky decisions in which both alternatives are good (plus-plus), or both seem bad (minus-minus). Or maybe there are plusses and minuses on both sides and they seem about equal. What am I to do in these double-bind situations?

Once I've submitted my will to God, prayed about the decision, and done everything else I can to discern His purpose and will, I need to just *make a choice and then go with it.* Sure, I'll choose wrong sometimes, but here's the good news: The Lord does not ask me to be always right. He asks only that I listen faithfully. "He who has an ear, let him hear what the Spirit says" (Revelation 2:7 NIV). And when I've sincerely tried to follow His will, the decision will be *spiritually* right.

It has been my experience, over the years, that if I am as honest with Him as I can be, and if I stay true to the best understanding of His will that I can discern, He will check my actions if they're wrong, or move heaven and earth to back me up if they're right. But I have to show I trust Him to do that. I have to make a decision and act on it.

A lovely Jewish legend says that when the Israelites reached the Red Sea and Moses struck the waters with his staff, nothing happened. Nothing at all . . . until one of the men put his foot into the water. Only then did the Sea part for the Israelites to walk through.[2]

My Lord is a good and faithful Father who has the firmness to assert His pattern in spite of my wrong turnings, when I allow Him to do it. He'll guide my choices, if I listen as best I can, trust Him, and follow the whisperings of the Holy Spirit.

3

God's Best Means Being True to Yourself

Learn to experience new-found freedom and satisfaction.

When I went away to college, I was determined to become the world's greatest actress. I'd had the leads in several high school plays, won dramatic reading contests, even received a drama scholarship to the University of Nebraska. I was sure I was destined for Broadway or Hollywood. Even my parents believed in my dream. My dad was especially excited about my acting future. Even though he was just a small-town doctor, he loved the theater and often took us to Omaha to see plays. I'll never forget how proud he was the afternoon the scholarship was announced. He went around telling everyone I was going to be the next Helen Hayes. Well, sure I was embarrassed, but deep down I desperately wanted to make that dream come true, for him as well as for myself.

But I didn't get good parts in college plays. The competition was too keen. (Once I played a talking ape. My parents made a special trip to Lincoln for the play and at the last minute the director cut my only line!) After three years of trying out and getting only mediocre parts, I finally had to face the fact that I wasn't going to be the world's greatest actress. In fact, I probably wouldn't be able to make a living in the theater at all. Discouraged and depressed, I decided to change my major.

But how I dreaded telling my parents! I felt like a real failure. The idea of losing my Dad's high esteem for me was almost more than I could bear. But when I went home for Christmas vacation that year, I forced myself to break the news. That moment of confessing my failure is deeply etched in my memory. When the words were out, silence fell on the room like a slap. I can still feel the dryness in my mouth and see the pattern in the couch fabric on which I ran my hands over and over, waiting for the lecture, waiting to be told, "You'll never get anywhere if you give up."

Then my father cleared his throat and said, "Well, Punk, I guess acting just isn't your song. I'm proud of you for facing that. Lots of people limp all the way through life trying to dance to the wrong tune. So, good for you! Now. Let's talk about finding the song that was written for you!"

It was the first time I'd thought about it that way. Could it be that in God's plan, there really was a song written just for me—a song that no one but I could sing, music that only I could dance to? Many years later, I was to find this passage in 2 Timothy 1:9 (NIV): "[God] has saved us and called us to a holy life—not because of anything we have done but because of his own purpose and grace. This grace was given us in Christ Jesus *before the beginning of time*" (italics mine). But where was I to look for that purpose? And how could I know when I'd found it?

Whose Song?

In the thirty-five years that have passed since I had that talk with my father, I've tried quite a few different tunes. Some of the notes have seemed right. Others haven't. But in searching for God's purposes for my life, one thing has become very clear. God sent me into the world with a song in my soul, and *to the extent that I'm true to my inner nature,* I will be singing that song. I believe this is true for every human being.

But what does being true to my inner nature *mean?* An incident that happened when I was just out of college gave me my first hint of that meaning. I'd been asked to teach a fourth grade Sunday school class, and I was very nervous about it. I remembered a church school teacher who had had a profound influence on my life, and I wanted so much to be the kind of mentor she had been. We all loved Miss Wilson, not only because she was a devout Christian and taught so well, but also because she had a delightful sense of humor. Somehow, that added such a sparkle to the class that it kept our interest at a high pitch.

In preparation for my first class, I spent hours pouring over books containing humorous anecdotes. I found a few that I thought the children would understand and that I could work in with the subject of the day's lesson. Well, you guessed it. They fell completely flat. As a comedienne, I'm a dismal failure. There were a few chuckles, but most of the kids looked at each other with raised eyebrows, as if to say, "What kind of goofy teacher did we get *this* time?"

"Well, how did it go?" asked my pastor when I saw him in the hall after class.

"Oh, Pastor," I said, on the verge of tears. "I guess I'm just not cut out to be a Sunday school teacher." I told him about Miss Wilson and her marvelous sense of humor . . . and about the jokes I'd tried that didn't work. "I thought God wanted me to teach this class, but now I'm not so sure. If only I could be the kind of teacher Miss Wilson was!"

My pastor put his hand on my shoulder and said something I've never forgotten. "God didn't ask you to be Miss Wilson. He asks only that you be Marilyn."

Once I gave up trying to be Miss Wilson, I found

that I had some special things that were uniquely mine to offer the class. We did lots of creative things, including baking a birthday cake for Jesus, acting out the Bible stories we studied, and making prayer notebooks. The kids loved it and so did I!

Last year, Rex and I had some business dealings with a young man who had been a student in that class. Jim said that after all these years, he still keeps a prayer notebook and that it's one of the most rewarding things he does. Oh! A teacher's dream come true!

Does my life really matter? It seems to me that the answer to that question is this: No matter how insignificant my talents may seem, if I develop and use the natural gifts God has given me (and every one of us does have special gifts), my efforts will have a positive effect. And who but God can know the reach of the smallest act that grows out of the person He created me to be? My life matters. Your life does, too.

Whose Values?

If the key is to be yourself, then how do you find out who you really are, deep inside? The first step is to discover those areas in which you are trying to live out what you really are *not*.

In my own search for God's purposes (always plural) for my life I had a number of false starts.

For many years, I lived largely by second-hand values, handed down to me by others. "You must be popular, join the best sorority, wear the latest fashions." Or, later, "Your success as a young married woman is measured by the number of social engagements on your calendar." But life is gradually teaching this reluctant student to question the *source* of her values.

This is especially important in the matter of vocation or calling. I needed to search for the script that God had written on my heart, instead of trying to fit myself into a role that someone else had written for me. When I gave up the hope of being an actress, I thought I'd like to become an English teacher. I *loved* words. Getting deep inside a piece of fine literature was one of my best spirit-lifters. But when I mentioned that to the man who had been my high school superintendent, he said, "Oh! You don't want to be an English teacher! They're a dime a dozen! What you really *should* do is become a speech and hearing therapist." His reasons were oh so logical: (1) I had already taken plenty of speech courses. By adding the required speech pathology and audiology classes, I could still graduate with my college class. (2) Speech and hearing therapy, a relatively new field at that time (the year was 1952), was wide open. I would have good job choices. And (3), the clincher, it paid more than English.

So I made the choice based on his advice, without considering what I really wanted. I didn't know that a few years deeper into life, graduating with my class wouldn't matter at all. It was not long before I realized that the demand for speech therapists didn't make me any more valuable to God or to myself, and the few extra dollars a month could never provide the feelings of satisfaction that come with doing work that you love. There are many fine speech pathologists who love their work (some of them are among my best friends), but I now know that, like acting, speech therapy was not my song. That experience taught me something, however, about finding God's will for my life. It's good to seek counsel from those you respect, but always take their advice home to your deepest self, to see if it's right for you.

Here are some things that have sometimes helped me to answer the question, Is it right for me? First, if I find that the course I've chosen causes me to keep looking over my shoulder for someone else's approval, then I need to question whether or not it's really what *I* want to be doing. Also, if it becomes terribly important for me to be better than someone else at what I do, that can be a clue that what I'm doing is not what God intended for me. Or if I'm unduly worried about the success of my work (outer results), that may be a sign that it's not the song God wrote on my heart.

On the other hand, when I'm on the right track, it seems that the work *itself* is reward enough. I can let go of what others may think of what I'm doing; I can give up trying to be better than someone else. I can do my best with what I have and stop worrying about results, because there's a deep inner knowing that *God* is taking care of the outcome. I've come to trust that if I ask, He will confirm me when I'm doing

His will, and He will not let me go in peace to follow a way that is not mine.

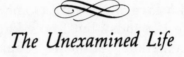

The Unexamined Life

One thing I've always known I wanted to be is a wife and mother. It's a role that's been very fulfilling to me. Snuggling up in a big chair with a child on my lap and a storybook in my hand, or kissing a hurt finger to make it well, or massaging Rex's back when he has a headache, or sharing quiet thoughts with him in front of the fireplace on a cold October night are among the things that truly feed my soul. But there were other things that I took for granted in the early years of our marriage, things I did just because they were what young married women did in the 1950s and 60s.

A certain moment is stamped in my consciousness like a footprint in fresh concrete. I was sitting in a friend's living room playing bridge for the third or fourth time that week. I can still hear the chatter of voices across the smoke-filled room as something clicked in my head. *Why am I doing this when for me it is nothing but sawdust?* The steady rounds of luncheons and parties, meetings, bridge clubs, and fancy desserts—all part of trying to keep pace on the social circuit—left me tired, spiritually hungry, and unfulfilled. Yet for years I had stayed on the merry-go-round, never once stopping to question *why.* I think

I'd convinced myself I liked it. But in that break-through moment, I had a sudden sense that I'd been betraying some sort of harmonious inner universe. I was completely out of touch with my own soul.

That day marked the onset of a transformation by self-discovery that was to lead me, ever so gently, into the presence of the Lord in a new and overturning way. It also led me back to college to start work on my master's degree (in English this time, dime-a-dozen or not!)

I don't think there's anything at all wrong with playing bridge, or with the other social activities I was involved in. What was wrong was that *I was doing them without asking myself and God if they were part of my song.* During that waking-up moment, I realized that I was meant to sing a different tune.

A young monk once went to his abbot and asked, "What good thing must I do to be saved?" The abbot answered, "Abraham was hospitable, and God was with him. Elijah lived alone, and God was with him. So whatever good thing you see *in your heart,* do that, and God will be with you."[1]

Choosing to Be Me

I believe that I come closest to fulfilling the purpose for which God created me when I am most nearly myself. For example, I'm not very good at planning and organizing, so when I was asked to be in charge of arrangements for the state Episcopal Church Women's centennial services, I declined. Again, as a singer, I'd make a good frog, so God forbid that I should ever try to join the choir! But I *do* enjoy reading aloud, so I serve as lay reader and lector every time I'm asked. (Could it be that even in the "false start" of all of those drama classes, God's plan was operating in my life, preparing me to serve in this way? How subtly do His patterns interweave!)

Somewhere I read that *the most common cause of despair is in not choosing to be oneself.* If I look at the times I've fallen into despair, I can see that it is often because I have denied or pushed down some basic characteristic of my own nature. For example, I do quite a bit of public speaking, and I thoroughly enjoy it. But last year, after leading a string of workshops and retreats and giving talks several times a week for many weeks, I began to feel as if my spirit had shriveled up and died within me. I was drained and depressed. Gradually, as I prayed through my darkness, it occurred to me that I had been denying an important aspect of my basic nature—the fact that I'm an introvert. Even though I enjoy being with people, I need more time alone than most people do. My energy comes from that private time, and if I don't get enough of it, I just simply run out of spiritual fuel. The result? Despair. My friend who's an extrovert says she gets depressed when she's *alone* too much and that being with people is the thing that recharges *her* battery. For each of us, it's a matter of being true to our own nature.

I think this choice to be oneself is one of the greatest responsibilities a person has in this world.

Maybe an analogy will show why. Every cell in the body has a purpose in line with its own inner nature, so that when each one is doing what it was created to do, the body operates in wholeness and harmony. In the same way, each person is created by God with a unique nature, and the events of life shape that uniqueness. As Paul put it in his letter to the Romans (12:4–7 RSV):

> For as in one body we have many members, and all the members do not have the same function, so we, though many, are one body in Christ. . . . Having gifts that differ according to the grace given to us, let us use them: if prophecy, in proportion to our faith; if service, in our serving; he who teaches, in . . . teaching. . . .

So I'll let others be the actresses, speech pathologists, socialites, organizers, and choir members. There are those in whom God has planted the right seeds for those vocations. I'll be as faithful as I can to my own callings of wife and mother, writer, lay reader, prayer group member, retreat leader. And yes, I'll schedule in some private time, without feeling guilty about it. I am convinced that to the extent that each of us lives true to our highest inner nature, God's plan for all humankind will be accomplished.

Successful People

Who are the people you think of as having truly made a difference in the world? Haven't they all insisted on being themselves? Jesus, who once turned down an offer to own "all the kingdoms of the world," chose to eat with sinners and harlots and tax collectors. When Henry David Thoreau was eight years old, someone asked him what he was going to be when he grew up. "Why," said the child, "I will be I!"[2] Years later, not a bit worried about being called an eccentric recluse, he gave the world a philosophy of simplicity that has changed lives. Albert Schweitzer could have had a lucrative urban medical practice but chose, instead, to go into the jungles of Africa to serve the suffering. These people found God's purposes by being true to their inner nature, by singing the song God put in their hearts. They must have listened well and then risked making the choice to live the leadings God gave them.

Sometimes I worry too much about what people think of me. At times I find it hard to express my differentness. Don't we all sometimes have these feelings of insecurity? Yet Jesus made it very clear that if I wanted to follow Him, I might not always fit in. "Blessed are you when people insult you, persecute you and falsely say all kinds of evil against you because of me" (Matthew 5:11 NIV). I'm still working on that one. I have a relative who calls prayer groups "kook meetings" and makes fun of my religious beliefs. When this gentleman is visiting, I'm often tempted to say I'm going to the grocery store when I leave for prayer group, or to skip my daily prayer times to avoid his sneering remarks. But then I remember how Jesus was mocked and spat upon, and I see that my little risk of being scoffed at is nothing. And I remind myself that *it's okay to be different.*

Think of the people you see every day. Isn't it true that the ones you most admire, those who are the most interesting to talk to, the most fun to be with, are the ones who are not afraid to be themselves? We have some friends whose life-style is definitely not determined by what others are doing. He's a retired college English professor who is writing the history of his World War II army division. He also writes mystical poetry, set in (believe it!) fox holes and old railroad depots. She is an outstanding contemporary poet who regularly publishes in the most prestigious journals. They walk everywhere, have never owned a car or a television set, and refused to accept the microwave oven they won in the church drawing because they "didn't need it." Every Tuesday afternoon and every Thursday morning, they walk many blocks to conduct Episcopal lay services at local nursing homes, and each Sunday during the summer, they hold services for travelers, at the Holiday Inn. I don't suppose anyone else in all the world could possibly have their unique combination of talents and interests, much less live true to them in this age of the machine. But I'll tell you one thing: If I were to make a list of people I know who are living truly *authentic* lives, this couple would be among the first to come to my mind.

So the overarching guide for finding God's purposes for your life is to live according to the nature that's your own. Be yourself.

But what if you still aren't quite sure how to become your real self?

The Search for You

"No one can know God who has not first known himself," observed the medieval scholar and writer Meister Eckhart.[3] The search for self is an essential part of the search for God. I believe it's also the best way to discover the song God imprinted on our hearts when He created us.

It may seem that looking inward is a rather self-centered thing to do. Actually it's a paradox—a seeming contradiction. It's only when I have found God within myself that I can begin to find Him and His purposes in my neighborhood or work place. "Keep a close watch on all you do and think. Stay true to what is right and God will bless you and use you to help others" (1 Timothy 4:16 TLB). "But when you pray, go away by yourself, all alone, and shut the door behind you and pray to your Father secretly, and your Father, who knows your secrets, will reward you" (Matthew 6:6 TLB). "Commune with your own heart upon your bed, and be still" (Psalm 4:4).

The search for your true self should be a God-directed activity, entered into prayerfully. Ask the Holy Spirit to be your guide. It may also be helpful to have a human guide, a devout, committed Christian who will help you in your inner search.

So how and where does this inward journey begin? What means of transportation are available? How much will it cost? What are the risks? Do we need a passport?

Let's take that last question first. The only passport we need is that we *must give ourselves permission to make the search within,* because it will, at times, run counter to some of the ways we've been programmed to think. When I first started spending time getting to know my inner self, there was an annoying voice in my head that kept saying things like, "You're not supposed to think about yourself." Or, "Why waste time writing down dreams? You've got more important things to do." Or, "What does all this matter, anyway?" But as I learned to ignore that nit-picky voice, I began to sense a certain *rightness* in the inward journey. And best of all, I gradually became more and more aware of my traveling companion, a young carpenter from Nazareth who once stood on a hill near Jerusalem and made the outrageous statement that "the kingdom of God is within you" (Luke 17:21).

Centering Prayer

There are many ways of discovering our inner nature. In the next chapter I'll discuss some of them, but here I want to talk about a form of prayer that enables me to find my inner self: *centering prayer.*

To center myself in prayer I usually start with a few minutes of mild physical exercise and some deep breathing to relax so I can sit still for a while. Then I sit down and lean slightly to the right and then to the left and then back to the center. Then I lean slightly forward, backward, and back to the center. Now my body feels centered. Next, I ask the question, "Who am I?" Then I begin to notice what thoughts drift through my mind. No matter what the thought is about—a worry about one of my children, a question about what to fix for dinner, a decision about my work—I deliberately let go of it, saying to myself, "This is not who I am." Then I wait quietly until another thought appears and repeat the procedure. I continue in this way for fifteen or twenty minutes, deliberately letting go of each thought. Gradually, there comes an awareness, from deep within, that *I am not any of the roles I play,* that *there is a deeper, truer self that is not defined by outer things.* I believe this is my spirit, the God-given spark of His nature that exists within every person, the light of Christ that was before all beginnings—"the true Light [who] arrived to shine on *every one* coming into the world" (John 1:9 TLB, italics mine). If you decide to try this type of prayer, I think you'll gain new perspective on who you really are.

A Surprising Answer

Another help in finding yourself is to sort out your feelings by writing them down. My daughter Karen was at a crossroad in her life a few years ago, with decisions to make in several areas. (By the way, don't limit your search for God's purposes just to career choices. His callings for you extend into every facet of your life.) Karen is a commercial artist, and she'd been offered a job in Minneapolis, with a promising future but not much freedom to be creative. She couldn't decide what to do. She had just started her own graphic arts business in Kearney, bought a small house, and fixed it up just the way she wanted it. Besides, there was a new young man in her life. She was madly in love with "Jim," but he had some problems she wasn't sure she could handle if she made a lifetime commitment. There were decisions to be made about further schooling, about pets, about friends, about organizations, about . . . well, you get the idea. Life seemed to be weighing very heavily upon Karen, and she began to feel depressed.

"I just don't know what to do about my life, Mom," she said one day. "I've been praying about it, but I don't seem to get any direction. I read a book on the will of God a while back, and the author said that God doesn't *have* plans for individual lives. He said that, in personal choices that don't involve morality, God doesn't really care which way you decide."[4]

"Come on now, Mom," said Karen, "tell me what you honestly think. Does my life *really* have any purpose as far as God is concerned? Does He give a hoot whether I take that Minneapolis job or not?"

I'm sure that Karen knew *my* answer to that question, but I also realized that it wouldn't be hers until she verified it for herself. So instead of giving a pat reply, I suggested that she do some writing about it. Karen has written "Letters to Jesus" since she was a teenager (maybe even before that), and has found it to be a very rewarding kind of prayer. So she started by writing out a prayer, asking the Lord to show her whether or not He had a purpose for her life. Then she just let all of her thoughts pour out onto the pages. She listed the people she most admired and found that they had some traits in common with one another, ones that were part of her nature, too. She made lists of her own assets and liabilities, of the things she most enjoyed doing, and of the activities she disliked. Then she wrote the statement, "The purpose of my life is . . ." and tried out different endings to the sentence.

After writing in this way off and on for several days, Karen called me one morning and said, "I got my answer, Mom. It came to me last night in bed. I know I didn't just think it up, because it was a complete surprise, not at all the answer I expected, or the way I would say things. As I was drifting off to sleep, these words seemed to float through my consciousness: 'Your purpose is to be an expression of Me. *The way* is by trusting yourself!'

"I was expecting an answer just for my present situation, but what I got is much bigger than that. I still don't know the answer to the Minneapolis question, or what to do about Jim, or whether or not to go back to school. But, Mom, *that's okay!* I know— absolutely *know*—that God has a purpose for my life. And I've found something deep within myself that I know I can trust to lead me in the right direction."

As I placed the phone back on the hook, something inside of this mother's heart fell on its knees.

Karen later decided against the Minneapolis job.

She's found that running her own business isn't easy, but Sunshine Signs is growing steadily, and so is Karen's ability to express her God-given artistic uniqueness. She also decided to break up with Jim, and it wasn't long before a delightful young man named Dave came into her life. She didn't have any trouble at all deciding that she wanted to become his wife.

His Will Revealed in Dreams, Images

Another way in which God sometimes reveals His purposes for individual lives is through dreams. In both the Old and the New Testaments, we see God regularly using dreams to direct people. Until about the thirteenth century, Christians took their dreams very seriously. Spiritual directors often recommended sleeping in front of the church altar for a night in order to solve a particularly perplexing problem. The solution was expected to come in the night's dreaming.

Then for a while, interpreting dreams fell out of favor. Today, through the influence of psychology, we know, as did Abraham and Solomon and Paul, that dreams can reveal our true selves—who we are and who we might become. God leads us throughout our sleeping as well as our waking hours. Listening to our dreams is one of the best channels for discovering God's will. We must truly become as little children if we are to knock on the door that is waiting to open to us. "For God speaks again and again, in dreams, in visions of the night, when deep sleep falls on men as they lie on their beds. He opens their ears in times like that, and gives them wisdom and instruction" (Job 33:14–16 TLB).

In the last several years, I have found that my dreams often help me make decisions. The symbols and the actions in the dream indicate the direction I should take.

A few years ago I felt led to write a book on Christian meditation. I was teaching in the English Department at Kearney State College at the time (yes, twenty-five years after I gave up the idea of becoming an English teacher, I was finally singing the song I'd heard in my heart as a young woman!), but began to sense that God's purposes for me were broadening out in other directions. Yet I was reluctant to ask for time off from teaching. Obviously I would have no income during that time. And would I be able to return to my teaching job after the book was finished? I knew, though, that I couldn't write this book in the short snatches of time between preparation and lectures and grading essays. What should I do?

While I was trying to make up my mind, I had a most vivid dream. I was pregnant, filled with the most amazing love for my dream child, and so happy to be getting ready for it—clothes, bathinette, crib, buggy, everything. Then suddenly I discovered myself in my living room surrounded by all the baby furniture—with no place to put it, because the whole house seemed to be filling up with junk of all kinds that kept crowding in on me. I looked into the crib for the baby—and found it full of stacks of student essays! In dismay I grabbed armfuls and tried to throw them out the window. But it didn't help. As soon as I'd throw a bunch out, more would come.

That was when I woke up, because I don't remember any more. But as I went over the details I had, it was not hard to interpret.

In my dream, the baby I was so thrilled and excited over stood for the book I wanted to write. The idea had been conceived and was growing in me—but I had no place for it in my life. The baby was being crowded out by stacks of essays, obviously standing for my teaching responsibilities. In the dream, I knew that the baby was far more important than the essays, so there was no question about what I had to do.

The next morning, after I had allowed the dream to speak to me, I talked to the head of the English department, and asked for a leave of absence in order to write the book. Not only did he grant me the leave, but he told me, "Remember we'll want you back next year."[5]

If you're looking for direction, if you're seeking God's purposes for your life, you might want to try keeping a dream diary. Dreams can be postcards from your higher self. They can help you discover who you really are, and in the process, you just might begin to hear the gentle, pure tones of a song written on your heart before you were born.

But What If You Still Aren't Sure?

What if, after praying about God's will for your life, spending time getting to know the person who lives inside your skin, listening carefully for God's guidance, and consulting a mentor (pastor, wise friend, or teacher), you're still not certain about your life's purposes? At that point, there's only one thing to do: make a decision and go for it. *Will to believe* that the direction you choose is God's leading. Go ahead. Risk making a mistake. That's a hundred percent better than living without purpose.

If settling on a purpose for your whole life is too overwhelming, begin by living purposefully for a day or an hour. My college speech teacher would never allow his students to begin a speech until we had handed him a piece of paper that read, "The purpose of this speech is . . ." I'm sure that our speeches were much more effective because of it. Sometimes, when I'm starting a new project (whether it's planning a retreat, preparing a new dessert recipe, or cleaning the storage room), I think of Dr. Lasse's requirement. If I take the time to put my purpose into words (either in my mind or on paper), I not only achieve better results but also find a greater amount of *satisfaction in the process* of achieving the goal.

Sometimes when I talk about living with purpose, someone protests, "But how could the things *I* do make a difference? All I can say is, 'These are the dishes I've washed.'" Or, "Come to the junk yard and I'll show you the cars I've repaired over the last thirty years." Or, "I'm eighty years old and in a wheel chair. What purpose could God have for my life now?" My answer is that God will take *whatever* you're able to do and use it to His purposes.

One woman who attends the Thursday morning services at Mt. Carmel nursing home in her wheel chair can't read the prayer book anymore, but she knows most of the prayers by heart anyway. Sometimes she talks to people who aren't there, and she often speaks out loud in the middle of the psalm or the homily. Once, when we didn't have an organist, the lay readers apologized to the little congregation for our off-key singing. Ismae said, "Well, it sounds beautiful in heaven, and that's all that counts." I left with a song in my heart that day—because of Ismae. Be true to your highest self, sing the song God gives you, no matter how insignificant it seems, and it *will* sound beautiful in heaven.

Nothing Is Ever Wasted

God's best for you means living each day to your very fullest and best. As with a great moving river, the currents of God's will in your life may change, and that's okay. A purpose-filled life is one of change, open expectation, and movement, not a static, stitched-up existence. That's such a freeing state of mind, because it helps me to let go of the things that don't work out, knowing that *no event is without meaning.*

One of my mother's favorite statements was, "Nothing is ever wasted." Once, when I'd spent hours on a report and the teacher didn't take up the papers, Mom said, "That's okay. You'll use it somewhere, sometime. Nothing is wasted." That material turned out to be just what I needed for an assignment in speech class during a very busy time the next year. Another time, when we were driving in the mountains looking for a particular picnic area, my dad took a wrong turn that put us an hour behind schedule. When he apologized for the wasted time, Mother said, "Now don't you worry about it, dear. Just think of all that beautiful scenery we would have missed if we'd gone the short way. Nothing is ever wasted, you know."

As soon as I discovered that I didn't really want to be a speech and hearing therapist, I moaned to Mother that my college degree had been wasted. I found her reply that "nothing is wasted" pretty hard to believe at that time. I didn't know, then, that my first child would have a speech problem, or that I would one day be asked to write a self-help book for the hearing impaired.[6]

Sometimes, when I'm sitting in a boring committee meeting, or washing the dishes, or working a crossword puzzle, or doing some other thing that seems to me or to others to be a waste of time, I hear the echo of my mother's voice reminding me that "nothing is wasted." And I know it's true. Over and over again, God has shown me that there is meaning in even the most mundane phases of my life.

When you're true to your deepest self, God's best will course through your life like a great streaming river. That doesn't mean that you'll always have everything you want or that life will be easy. What it does mean is that you can let go, trust, and flow with His will, and that there will be meaning and purpose in every aspect of your life.

Finding God's Best for You

Open to God in prayer and let His Spirit guide you through each day.

During the latter years of my parents' forty-seven-year marriage, they got so that they talked alike, acted alike, even *looked* somewhat alike. There was a certain tilt of the head, lift of the brow, inflection of the voice that always reminded me of the other, no matter which of them was speaking. They could order for each other in a restaurant, buy clothes for each other, even finish each other's sentences. After they had lived together so long, they each knew the other's mind almost as well as their own.

Such intimate closeness, whether in marriage or friendship, doesn't develop when we're making small talk at a party or discussing the day's work with our co-workers. It develops when we spend time with another person, gradually letting down our defenses and sharing our deepest hopes and dreams, our fears and even our pain. It was my parents' everyday companionship and deep sharing through the years of their marriage that made them so close.

Perhaps you have sensed, as I have, a certain superficiality to the way most of us live. Some of that comes from our lack of intimacy with other people. We long for an intimate friendship that will fill an inner emptiness. But perhaps you've also had flashes of awareness of a glorious reality that shimmers beyond your physical senses, and you yearn for more. Deep calling unto deep is how the Psalmist describes it (Psalm 42:7).

Wouldn't it be great to know you're in God's presence, to have an intimate friendship with Him? It can happen. When we listen to that deepest part of ourselves and begin to let God into it, we will have begun the journey to that kind of intimacy. And we will begin to know His personal will for us.

The key to knowing God's will is daily communion with Him. When we spend time with the Lord daily, gradually we develop an inner sense of His will. Then when decisions need to be made, we are able to make them more easily, because we know intuitively what He would have us do in each situation. As in a good marriage, it's the daily companionship that creates that kind of perceptive intimacy.

How can we have this? As with any friendship, going to God's house every week will help. But it's

really in the day-in, day-out companionship that
closeness develops. By spending time with God
every day, you and I can develop the intimacy with
Him that Paul speaks of when he says, "We have the
mind of Christ" (1 Corinthians 2:16).

Development of this inner sense of God's will
doesn't happen overnight. There are no sure-fire
techniques for discovering God's will or for guaran-
teeing accuracy! Some saintly people may be able to
stay centered in God's presence all the time, but most
of us float in and out. And when that deep knowing
comes upon us, it is always a free gift, pure grace,
unearned and undeserved. "The wind blows wherever it pleases. You hear its sound, but you cannot
tell where it comes from or where it is going. So it is
with everyone born of the Spirit" (John 3:8 NIV). We
can't learn God's will by twisting His arm.

*Yet there are certain things we can do to help ourselves be
open to receive that grace.*

Because the soil isn't very rich around our house
in Kearney, we've never been able to grow much. But
last year Rex and I spaded up a small area, added
some peat and other soil nutrients, and planted a few
tomatoes, peppers, and cucumbers. We weeded and
watered, and, wonder of wonders, the plants grew
and produced some fine vegetables! We did not make
those plants grow. All we did was provide the right
conditions so that *God* could give the increase.

It's the same with our spiritual lives. There are
certain things we can do to prepare the soil of our
souls so that God can plant His will within us. I call
them *prayer enablers.* They are activities that will en-
able us to hear God and to know His will.

Some Support Systems[1]

Regularity in prayer is the number one key to knowing and living God's best in our daily lives. But if you're like I am, even though you intend to pray regularly, you sometimes find it hard to stick to that commitment. Because I often have trouble disciplining myself, I've had to work out some support systems to keep me steady in my prayer life.

One thing that helped me in the beginning was to *make a prayer covenant.* When I decided to do this, I took my Bible and a notebook, went into the bedroom, and closed the door. I sat down with my Friend Jesus and asked Him to help me set a realistic prayer goal. Half an hour twice a day seemed within reach for me. You'll have to decide what's reasonable for you. It would be better to start out with one prayer period a day—even a ten-minute one—and stick with it, than to try for two or three and give up in frustration. You can always add a second or third period, or take more time, after daily prayer becomes an established habit.

Another thing that really helps me is to *schedule my prayer time into my day* in the same way that I would a business appointment or a lesson. It's essential to choose the time when you're most alert. I know quite a few people who set their alarms fifteen or twenty minutes early in the morning and have their time with God before breakfast. I tried that but found I was so groggy, my mind kept wandering. I'm just not an early morning person. Besides (I might as well admit it), my stomach growled and all I could think about was toast and coffee! I've found that 11:00 A.M. and 10:00 P.M. work best for me.

When I first started scheduling time for prayer, there were six of us living at home and I was a part-time teacher, a correspondent for a national newspaper, a Sunday school teacher, and a free-lance writer. I thought surely something would have to go, but once I got into the habit of daily prayer, I discovered an astonishing thing. The more regular I was about keeping my appointments with God, the more I got done! I think it's because an internal ordering takes place during prayer that carries over into daily activities.

It's helpful, also, to *establish a regular place for prayer,* so when you enter that special room and sit in that same chair, your mind automatically begins to tune in to the Lord. It should be a place where you can be alone without being interrupted. Now that our daughter Karen is married, her room has become my prayer room, but you don't have to have a spare bedroom. Be creative and you'll find a place. A curtained-off portion of a basement or garage, a laundry room or back porch, or a walk-in closet could become a holy place for you, if it is graced by daily prayer. I have a friend who lives in a small apartment with her husband and two little children. She does her praying in her parked car.

Once you've found your time and place, it will help if you can *minimize distractions.* Take the phone off the hook or ask whoever's home to take calls. If you're alone, you may want to put a note on the door. It can be very simple: "Please do not disturb between 11:00 and 11:30 A.M. Thank you." If you can't find a quiet place to pray, buy a pair of earplugs. I use mine when my prayer time coincides with a TV program Rex is watching, or the dogs are barking, or the grandchildren are playing in the next room.

A little rule that has helped me stay faithful to my prayer commitment is this: *shorten instead of skipping.* On those days when you absolutely cannot get in your full prayer time, you can at least offer an abbreviated prayer. I found out, during a crammed-full week, that skipping one prayer period made it that much more tempting to skip again the next day. That was when I decided that five minutes with the Lord are better than no time at all. Just be sure you shorten only on the days when that's the sole alternative to skipping prayer.

Another thing that has helped me is to *keep a prayer diary.* It takes just minutes to record the date and any insights that come from time spent with the Lord. I like to note specific prayer requests and people I've prayed for. When I look back through my diary, I'm always amazed at the surprising ways the Lord has answered my prayers. It makes me very much aware of the steady movements of His Spirit in my life, and of the patterns that make up His best for me.

I've found that a very good aid to staying faithful about daily prayer is to *find a prayer partner.* It should be someone you feel close to, who is committed to the Lord and who will join you in regular prayer. Agree on a daily time. My friend Carolmae and I meet periodically to pray; on days between, we signal each other with one ring on the phone when it's prayer time. We've been doing this for about seven years now, and it's helped us both to be more faithful to our prayer covenants.

I've also learned to *give thanks for dry, inarticulate periods in prayer.* If your time with the Lord sometimes seems barren and you think nothing at all is happening, remind yourself that this is precisely the time when the Lord is working behind the scenes to prepare you to come closer to Him. It's true! Dryness in prayer creates a thirst for God, making us ready to answer the call of the Spirit: "The Spirit and the bride say, 'Come.' Let each one who hears them say the same, 'Come.' Let the thirsty one come—anyone who wants to . . . come and drink the Water of Life without charge" (Revelation 22:17 TLB). *Be faithful through the dry times, and He'll draw you closer to Him.*

I'll admit that I still let other responsibilities crowd out my prayer time now and then, and sometimes I still find it hard to discipline myself in prayer, but the lapses are gradually getting farther apart. And it's become very clear to me that, when I'm regular in prayer, I have a much better sense of the direction God wants me to go, minute by minute, hour by hour, day by day.

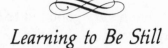

Learning to Be Still

So yes, it's very important to be regular about prayer. But then comes the question: What do you *do* during your daily time with the Lord? Maybe you already pray every day but still don't feel that you have a good sense of God's best for you. I do think it's possible to sit in prayer every day without coming to know God better. Maybe it's because we have a tendency to want to monopolize the conversation. Maybe it's because we are too impatient. Maybe we're looking for some dazzling experience instead of waiting for God Himself.

Instead, during part of our prayer time, we need to let ourselves become like a willow tree on a river bank, just sitting quietly soaking up God's presence. Just as a tree soaks up water from a flowing river, the presence of the Holy Spirit seeps into our souls when we're still before God. Scripture teaches us, again and again, to value stillness. "Be still, and know that I am God" (Psalm 46:10). "He leadeth me beside the still waters" (Psalm 23:2). "Commune with your own heart upon your bed and be still" (Psalm 4:4). "Come away by yourselves . . . and rest a while" (Mark 6:31 RSV).

When you practice stillness before God every day, you'll begin to realize that there is a center of His infinite wisdom within you that protects, maintains, and sustains. Once you've become aware of that, it will begin to flow out through you, directing your actions, drawing to you what you need, leading you to be at the right place at the right time.

When I'm regularly spending time just being present with the Lord in love (which means simply being still, being open, coming to Him empty), these things really do happen. For example, last Thursday, John needed to borrow my car, so he dropped me off at the church for prayer group. He was supposed to pick me up at 5:00, but when I came out of the church, he wasn't there. Everyone but Carolmae had left. She offered to take me home, but I didn't want to leave, because I had no way to let John know. So Carolmae and I waited in her car. It turned out that she desperately needed to talk, and I was able to put her in touch with exactly the person she'd been needing to contact, in connection with a serious problem. If John's car hadn't been on the blink, if he hadn't been late picking me up, if the church hadn't been locked, Carolmae and I would have gone our separate ways after prayer group.

Now, you might say that such things are simply coincidence. But it's an interesting fact that "coincidences" like that happen again and again to people who maintain daily companionship with the Lord. And, as former archbishop William Temple once wrote, "When I stop praying, coincidences stop happening."[2] I have found that to be true, too!

When Your Mind Wanders During Prayer

In order to know God better, a portion of every prayer time needs to be set aside for just being present with Him in love. That's hard to do because our minds are so constructed that words and thoughts rush in without being invited, to fill up any empty spaces.

One thing that has helped me with this is to go in my imagination to a special place where I've experienced God's presence in the past. Perhaps you can remember a time and place in which you felt the wonder and the beauty of God surrounding you in a deeply moving way. We have a cabin in the Colorado Rockies that has been in my family since 1912, so I've spent time there almost every summer of my life. It's only a fifteen-minute hike from the cottage to a little spring where we've always gone to get our drinking water.

A few years ago, the village put in its own water purification plant, so the trip to the spring isn't necessary any more. And yet I keep making it. I'll probably do it for as long as my legs and feet will take me there, because being in that spot somehow connects me with that which is beyond myself. No matter how burdened I may feel, no matter what heaviness I carry, no matter how alienated from myself I seem, when I push through the leafy shrubs that hide the spring from the road and work my way down to the creekside, all the layers of tension I've carried with me peel away. There's something about that pure, crystal cold water that makes my world fresh and clean and new. And I seem to hear a voice echoing across the centuries: "If any one thirst, let him come to me and drink" (John 7:37 RSV).

So when I'm trying to still my mind during the listening part of my prayer time, I often go to that mountain spring in my imagination, and it seems to put me in touch with God's presence.

Another thing that helps me to enter the stillness is to just quietly say the name of the Lord, over and over, as I sit there. "Jesus, Lord Jesus . . . Jesus, Lord Jesus . . . Jesus, Lord Jesus . . . Jesus, Lord Jesus . . ."

This kind of prayer seems to open up the door to my inner

mind. Perhaps that's the door Jesus referred to when He said, "Behold, I stand at the door, and knock; if any one hears my voice and opens the door, I will come in to him and eat with him, and he with me" (Revelation 3:20 RSV).

And here's good news: You can carry this inner stillness away from your scheduled prayer times, right into your daily living. While waiting in a grocery line, or when you're restless in the night, or as you're awaiting your turn to pay your toll on a freeway, just begin silently repeating the name of the Lord. You'll be surprised at the difference it will make in your day.

This waiting on God, being silent before Him, simply being with Him in love is one of the most important things we'll ever learn. It is the key to "putting on the mind of Christ." It is the channel through which God's best can flow through our lives, today, tomorrow, and always. If you sincerely want to know God's will, spend part of every prayer time just being a river willow, planted near Him, soaking up His presence. Then carry it with you into your daily life.

Praying with the Bible

Another way to open the channel so that God's will can flow through your life is to pray with your Bible.

Several years ago, I attended a Scriptural Prayer Retreat that made the Bible come alive for me. I found out that praying with the Bible is not the same thing as Bible reading or Bible study. Here's how you can do it. Choose a *short* Bible passage (no more than three or four verses). If you use a daily devotional guide, you may use the reading for the day, or you could just start reading a book of the Bible, a few verses each day. Begin by dedicating the time to the Lord and asking Him to speak to you through that passage. Then read it, one word at a time, *very slowly*, allowing each word to float in your mind for several seconds before going on. When the Lord stops you (and He will!), just quietly rest in His presence with those words as your prayer. You may feel led to converse with Him at that point, possibly asking what He wants to say to you in the passage. Know that *the message is specifically for you at that moment in your life.* Our Lord might use the very same passage to say something completely different to another person, or to you at another time. You'll soon discover how very personal this kind of prayer is. You will know what it means to actually encounter God Himself, in His holy Word.

Then choose a word or phrase from the passage to take away with you. Carry it in your heart throughout the day, returning to it often for refreshment and renewal. You will be surprised to find that those words are exactly what you need, in some situation that arises during your day.

A few weeks ago, my reading was from the Book of Deuteronomy, chapter 31, verses 6 through 8 (JB). The parts that seemed directed especially to me that day were: "Be strong, stand firm . . . your God is going with you; he will not fail you or desert you. . . . [He] himself will lead you; he will be with you;

he will not fail you or desert you. Have no fear, do not be disheartened by anything." During my prayer time, I didn't really know *why* the Lord had chosen those words for me, but as I sat there, soaking them in through my roots, I began to feel wonderfully strong and capable of meeting whatever the day might bring. My take-away words for the day were the first four: "Be strong, stand firm."

Before the day was over, I knew why I had those words in my heart. About four o'clock in the afternoon, my son John started begging me to let him cash in some of his college savings to buy a piece of stereo equipment. John is a very determined young man, and I am often putty in his hands. Lack of assertiveness with my children has always been a problem for me. I started arguing with him and trying every kind of persuasion I could think of, but after a while, I had the sinking feeling that I was about to give in, even though I knew I shouldn't. At that moment, those words from my morning Scriptural prayer time rose to the surface of my mind. "Be strong, stand firm." Instantly, I knew that I was not alone, that a very strong, stable, solid, loving Father backed me up.

My voice was calm and steady as I said, "I'm sorry, John. The answer is no. There will be no further discussion about it."

John looked at me as if I were someone he'd never seen before. Then he shrugged and said, "Well, okay." You could have knocked me over with a feather.

Praying with my Bible has taught me, over and over again, that *God's will is not something I have to seek "out there" but rather something that flows out from me, when I hold the Word within.* The Holy Spirit keeps using my daily Scripture readings to guide me in unexpected ways. He will do it for you, too, whether your need is to stand firm with your teenager, or to receive guidance about a business decision, or to be led to the right doctor. Pray with your Bible daily and you'll discover it for yourself!

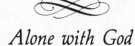

Alone with God

In recent months, my son John's life has become so busy with school, extracurricular activities, and friends that I practically have to make an appointment with him if I need to talk privately about something. When John is home, it seems that there are always several friends here, too. During the last few weeks, however, the steady stream of teenage boys around our house has slowed down drastically. The reason? A pretty little blonde named Marjorie (John calls her GiGi). My son has fallen in love, and even the guys know that a girl and a boy need time alone together. It's the only way to get to know each other.

It's like that with God, too. *Our knowledge of God's will increases within us in the measure that our love for Him increases.* And how does love increase? Only by spending time alone together. In the Gospels we see Jesus taking time, regularly and periodically, to withdraw from the multitudes, and even from His disciples, to spend time alone with His Father. He tells us to do the same: "Come away by yourselves to a lonely place, and rest a while" (Mark 6:31 RSV).

Too often, however, there's a nagging voice inside me that keeps saying things like, "When you get all your work done, *then* you can go away by yourself." Or, "Isn't that kind of selfish of you to want time alone? After all, you're a wife and mother." Or, "A whole day? I couldn't possibly spare *that* much time!" Or, "Just as soon as I finish this project, I'll take some time." Of course, by then there's something else that urgently needs to be done.

Lately, however, I've started talking back to that voice. I've been *scheduling in* twenty-four hours of alone-with-God time at least every other month. This twenty-four-hour sabbatical has been a life-changing discovery. Sometimes I go to a retreat center in a nearby town, where there's a little cottage nestled among the tall pines. Inside is a little wood-burning stove, cushions and a sleeping bag, an old-fashioned pitcher and wash basin, a chair, a desk with an open Bible, a thermos of drinking water, and a loaf of nutritious bread.

The first time I went there, I was a little nervous about it, but as soon as I'd settled in, it seemed as though I'd come home. As I spent my time reading from the Bible, writing in my prayer journal, and just being aware of God's presence with me, layer after layer of emotional stress I hadn't even known I was carrying around just gently peeled away. For the first time, I really understood Paul's words in 2 Corinthians 5:17 (RSV), that anyone "in Christ . . . is a new creation; the old has passed away, behold, the new has come."

About midway in that first sabbatical, it occurred to me that it was the first time in my whole life that I'd ever spent twenty-four hours without seeing or talking to another person. That fact is rather amazing, I think, in a fifty-five-year stretch. But there was absolutely no sense of loneliness—only a gently increasing awareness of a precious inner Presence that nested on my heart like a bird.

Since then, I've returned to that little cottage many times, but I've also taken twenty-four-hour sabbaticals in our camper. A motel room would work, or even a tent in nice weather. If you just simply can't get out at all, maybe you could get a change of scene by spending a day with the Lord in a room you don't usually spend much time in. Or if that's impractical for you, there is always the priceless asset of your imagination. By an act of will, decide to journey away from your surroundings. Let your mind roam until it finds a pleasant place to be. Arrange it so that you can take a vacation from your daily work routines. (And don't feel guilty about it! Periodically getting out of the fast traffic lanes and away from the things that clutter up your life will make you a *better* wife or husband, mother or father, worker or employer—in fact, a better person.) A minister I know says that he makes it a point now and then to "waste time with God." Well, of course the time isn't wasted, but maybe thinking of it that way will help you give yourself permission to do it. I hope you'll try it. It's a very good way to open to God so that you can begin to sense His will for you.

Walk with a Special Friend

Sometimes, when the weather's decent, I take walks. They've become times of private companionship with my Friend, Jesus. If you've never taken a prayer walk, I'd like to invite you to do so. It's a very good way to open to God. God has never spoken to me in audible words, but He often makes Himself understood through symbols. Some of the most vital messages I've received from Him have come to me during my prayer walks.

A prayer walk is like a secret meeting just between two friends. On this walk you will know Him by His voice, which may sound like a robin's song, or like rustling leaves, or like children playing. His voice might even come to you in such unexpected sounds as a train going by in the distance or a car horn honking. Consider that every sound you hear, as you walk with your Friend, is His voice speaking to you.

Be aware that God is in all things. Perhaps you'll see Him in the brightly colored leaves of autumn, or in the spring tulips, or in the blue sky with its soft clouds. In the city you can sense the Lord's presence in the rhythms of the people walking, in the wonder of so many different faces, in the tall buildings that seem to reach toward heaven.

When you first go outside, I'd like to suggest that you look at the sky. It will break you out of your limited world by putting you in touch with God's vastness. Then look all around you, as you've never looked before. Do a 360 degree sweep of the horizon. Look in places you usually miss when you drive by them in the car—deep within the grass, or at a small section of gravel, or at the minute sparkling particles of glass imbedded in the concrete of the sidewalk. Try to look with fresh eyes, seeing as if for the first time. I think that's what Jesus meant when He said that we must "receive the kingdom of God as a little child" (Mark 10:15). *Wherever* you walk, look with love, and you will see God.

Allow yourself to feel the breath of the Holy Spirit touching you, in the air that brushes over you. Then take in a deep breath, and notice the scent in the air. Newly cut grass, flowers, dry leaves, even dust are all parts of God's holy earth and can help you to enter His presence.

If you're in need of guidance, you might want to mentally repeat the words of Psalm 25:4 as you walk: "Show me thy ways, O Lord; teach me thy paths."

Close friends often give each other little gifts as tokens of their love—something that can be carried away to remind them of one another when they are apart. Maybe your eternal Friend has a gift for you this day. Go out, expecting to receive, and when the Lord presents His gift, you will know it.

One night after I'd had an argument with my husband and I was feeling very low in self-esteem, I stepped on something on the sidewalk, a couple of blocks down the street. It was a broken piece of green glass. Because it spoke to me of my own brokenness, I knew it was my Friend's gift for me, a sign that He knew how I was feeling, that even He had felt that way at times. When I got home, I placed the broken glass on the kitchen windowsill and forgot about it. The next morning as I was eating breakfast, a glint of something caught my eye. The piece of broken glass looked like a shining emerald there, transformed by the rays of the sun shining through it! Then I realized that I am like that piece of glass. When the SON shines through me, my brokenness is transformed!

When participants in a retreat bring back their gifts from a prayer walk and share with the group the message the Lord has given them through His gift, there is an amazing variety both of gifts and of messages—from leaves to seed pods to rocks and pieces of gravel, even bottle caps. Each gift speaks to a special need of the person receiving it. Often the prayer walkers go past the object and then are drawn back to it.

"As I walked past this old lilac bush," Becky told us, "a branch scratched my arm and broke off. I thought, *Could this be my gift? Oh, surely not that dead-looking thing!* As I walked on, I kept thinking about that branch and it just seemed to pull me back. Finally, I *had* to go back and pick it up, and as I held it in my hand and asked God what He wanted to say to me, I suddenly *knew!* I've been cutting myself off from Him since my husband died. That's why I've been so depressed! I sat down in the soft grass under the bush and for the first time in months, I felt the Lord's presence, protecting me, loving me. It seemed that I even sensed Brad's presence there, too. I know now that the best way to stay linked with Brad is to stay close to Christ!"

Not all gifts are tangible. Sometimes the gift is an insight or a spiritual uplift. Recently on a prayer walk in New York City, my gift was this: With each block, I noticed that fewer people were avoiding my eyes the way strangers do. Instead, eyes began to meet mine, and expressions sometimes changed from worried or frowning to a quick smile. I realized that when I walk with my Friend Jesus, *His* light begins to shine out, touching others, and they respond. Now what gift could surpass that?

Maybe you'll decide to have a walk with your Friend Jesus today. It's a wonderful way to open your inner door to Him and to others.

Affirmative Prayer

In the past thirty years, there has been a great burgeoning of interest in the teaching that thoughts actually have a direct influence on events and circumstances. It is life-transforming to discover that the thoughts and images we hold in mind do tend to materialize, whether they be positive or negative. It makes perfect sense, then, to pay attention to one's thoughts and thereby increase the likelihood of attracting positive experiences into our lives. It's a practical way to increase our ability to pray believing, according to Jesus' recommendation in Mark 11:24 (NIV): "Therefore I tell you, whatever you ask for in prayer, believe that you have received it, and it will be yours." Focusing on mental images of the things and circumstances we desire is a very effective form of prayer.

Affirmations are positive statements repeated as prayers, such as "All things are working together for good in my life today" (from Romans 8:28). Positive imaging is holding a picture in one's mind of the perfect answer to your prayer. Affirmative prayer and positive imaging are an important part of my prayer life, but I think that the very effectiveness of these forms of prayer makes it absolutely essential that I continually ask for God's direction and seek to know His will as I pray.

I must be very careful never to allow myself to think that the power is mine. Recently, a woman who had studied imaging prayer said to me, "We couldn't find a house we liked that was within our budget, so I started visualizing our perfect home at the ideal price. Within a week, my imaging brought us just the house we'd been looking for!" No. Her imaging didn't bring the house. Visualization helped her to pray believing, but it was God who made the connection between the family and their dream home.

There's also a strong temptation, with these powerful tools for living, to focus on getting things or bringing certain circumstances into one's life, rather than on learning to know God better and to love Him more. *Always, the focus of my prayer life should be on God and not on the events and conditions of my life.* So before using imaging prayer, I need to center myself in the Lord, carrying Jesus' familiar words in my heart, "Seek ye first the kingdom of God, and His righteousness; and all these things shall be added unto you" (Matthew 6:33).

In an effort to think positively, it's important to be aware of any negative feelings you might have, and to deal with them instead of swallowing them. When I first started reading books on positive thinking and affirmative prayer, I went around all day repeating affirmations, such as "I am healthy in body, soul, and spirit," or "I am at peace with everyone I meet." This was all to the good, except for one thing. After a few weeks of this, the migraine headaches (which I'm prone to anyway) became more and more frequent. I tried to combat them by affirming, "I am free from pain and I feel great," but they only became more severe and frequent. My doctor sent me to a counselor, who explained what I'd been doing to myself. I was denying my negative feelings, but they were still there. In fact, they were *more* menacing to my emotional and physical well-being now, because they had gone underground.

Since then, when I practice affirmative prayer, I try to first admit any negative emotions I may have and deal with those by talking them out, by writing them down, or by going for a brisk walk. Only then do I start my affirmations. The important thing is to get the painful feelings out instead of denying them.

Keeping these few cautions in mind, we can all use imaging and affirmations to help us to *pray believing.* This will help open the door for God's generous and perfect will to work in our lives.

When You're Feeling Empty

Sometimes, however, no matter how faithful you've been in prayer, no matter how intimate your relationship with your God, there are days when a steely gray dullness sets in and life seems to lose its lustre. I went through a time like that recently. The day was cold and gray. No wind, no rain, no sun. There was nothing seriously wrong in my life . . . just a bunch of little things nagging at my sense of well-being.

About three o'clock in the afternoon, I forced myself to put on my old green coat, stocking cap, and gloves and walk through the little valley behind our house, to Kearney Lake. As I tramped over the winter-flattened prairie grass, the bare trees seemed like skeletons, lifeless against the dull sky. Somewhere in the distance, I heard the whack of a ball against a bat, and the slowly receding squeals of children playing.

The lake was the lowest I'd ever seen it, with great gray swaths of dry, cracked ground all around its edges. The water was a dull, mud-green, absolutely motionless. From somewhere overhead, I heard the thin, shrill cry of a lonely bird. The sound was long and frail and fading, like the sound of a single held note on a piccolo. There was an emptiness, a forsakenness in the scene that corresponded with the landscape of my heart and the heaviness in the pit of my stomach. I thought, *I have so much, and yet I feel so poor.*

Almost immediately, from somewhere in the

back of my heart, came Jesus' words, "Blessed are the poor in spirit." I'd never understood what those words meant. Could it be that the emptiness I was feeling that day was somehow a blessing? As I plodded along the dry edges of the lake, I stopped resisting the hollow feeling within and allowed myself to give in to it. Gradually, my neck and stomach muscles started to relax. I began to notice little fringes of greenness along the water's edge and delicate leaf-buds on the cottonwoods. And slowly the slightest bit of greenness began to finger its way gently into that gray space within me. Not much. Just a little. But it was enough to give me hope and lift my spirits. It helped me to remember that *it's all right to be empty sometimes. Because only the empty can be filled.*

I think that *is* what it means to be poor in spirit—to be empty before God. We don't like to feel empty, but Jesus says that when we're in need and we know it, that's when we can be filled. "Blessed are the poor in spirit: for theirs is the kingdom of heaven" (Matthew 5:3). Surrendering to emptiness, when it comes, can be a way of opening to Him.

The prayer enablers I've described in this chapter have helped me to tune in to God and to begin to sense His will for me. They've gradually increased my confidence that life is truly meaningful and that I can trust the Holy Spirit to lead me in every circumstance of my life. You will have the same assurance, when you listen for His voice in the wind and the sea and the city streets . . . and in the silence of your heart laid bare before Him. When you've chosen the prayer enablers that seem right for you and started to practice them, you'll find yourself opening to God in fresh new ways. As your daily companionship with Him grows, you'll begin to know that in giving you Himself, He has given you everything.[3]

God's Best Means Saying Yes to Life

Find new meaning in disappointments and failure; expect the best, moment by moment.

When I was a teenager, I went through a period of questioning my faith. Luckily, Aunt Alta wasn't afraid of questions. One cold, sunless day in early spring, Aunt Alta and I were doing dishes together in the kitchen of her big old farmhouse, when we got to talking about Easter and I blurted out the question, "But how do we *know* Jesus really came back from the dead? I know the Bible says He did, but how can we

be sure that those people didn't just *say* they saw
Him? It was all such a long time ago."

Aunt Alta dried her hands on her big flour-sack
apron. "Yes, it was a long time ago," she said, "but
this day is as full of meaning as that day of resurrection was. In fact, *this moment is as meaningful as any
moment in all eternity!* Come with me a minute."

I followed Aunt Alta out the back door, down
the rickety wooden steps, and across the backyard, to
a clump of gray, dead-looking bushes by the fruit
cellar door. An icy March wind whipped the
branches back and forth as she reached down and cut
off a few pieces about eighteen inches long. When
we were back in the house, she got a milk-glass vase
out of the pantry, filled it with water, placed the
branches in it, and put it on the table by the west
window in the parlor. The "bouquet" looked like a
bunch of bony-fingered skeletons sitting there, so
stark and bare.

But in three days, those dead-looking twigs
blossomed into a profusion of bright yellow, glori-
ously living flowers, even though the bushes outside
were still gray. Then Aunt Alta explained to me that
just as the forsythia bloomed when we brought it
into the house, I needed to bring Christ into the
living room of my life. If I'd do that, she said, I would
know, *firsthand,* that the resurrection was true, because His living presence would blossom within me.
Over the years, I've experienced the truth of that.
The more I'm able to include Christ in my daily
routine, whether I'm brushing my teeth or dusting or
preparing a talk, the more real His presence becomes
for me.

Rex and I have lived in several different homes since we were married, and one of the first things I do when we move into a new place is to plant forsythia bushes. And every spring, while the days are still gray and blustery, I bring in several sprigs and put them in a vase. It's become a ritual for me, a very special reminder to try to keep Christ in the living room of my life. One of the best ways to be aware of Him is to watch and listen for His presence in the little and big events of every day, reminding myself that every place, every moment is an opportunity to discover God's best for me.

During the past few years, I've made a deliberate effort to pay closer attention to the ordinary events of my daily life, to see what meanings I might find there. As I did this, a most astounding thing began to happen. I began to see meaningful messages in such commonplace things as a kinked garden hose, a discarded fern, and a trapped butterfly. Looking over the shoulders of art students as they painted the lake scene near our house provided me with a lesson in seeing truth from more than one point of view. Trying to iron a shirt when I'd forgotten to plug in the iron helped me to see why I was having such a hard time smoothing out the wrinkles in a certain relationship. (I hadn't brought Christ into the problem. I was unplugged from my heavenly Power Source!)

Since I've been trying to search out the deeper meanings in ordinary incidents, I've become convinced that daily circumstances are one of God's best ways of communicating His will to me! There *is* meaning in most (maybe all!) of life's happenings, if I look for it. The meaning is not usually obvious.

Very often it's symbolic. I like Madeleine L'Engle's statement that "the Holy Spirit does not hesitate to use any method at hand to make a point to us reluctant creatures."[1] Listening to the messages that come through ordinary happenings is a very effective way to stay in touch with God's will.

The Lord said to the prophet Amos: "Behold, I will set a plumbline in the midst of my people Israel" (Amos 7:8). A plumbline is a weight on a string that is used to make sure the walls of buildings are straight. It serves as a guide for the builder. Every part of the work that rises from the ground is checked and set according to the plumbline. My dictionary also gives this definition of the word *plumb:* "To discover the facts or contents of; fathom; solve; understand." I think it's worth noting that the Lord did not tell Amos He was setting a plumbline in heaven . . . or even in the synagogue. He said He was setting it right in the midst of His people. When I watch and listen for God's messages in the little daily things, they serve as a plumbline for the building of my months and years. I believe that this is one way He directs the overall building of my life.

We can all look for the significance of daily experiences. All that's needed is a desire to know God's will and a deliberate effort to look for it "in the midst of my people." It can be found in many ways: by mining one's memories, by reflecting on each day's events, by tracing circumstances back through the strings of cause and effect, by looking for symbolic meaning in objects and incidents, by becoming aware of unexpected blessings and apparent coincidences.

Memory Mining

Many people feel that nothing particularly meaning-ful happens to them, that they really don't know much about the art of living. I used to feel that way, too. But when I began to think about the people I'd known during my growing-up years, I found that many of them had taught me valuable lessons about how to live more fully—my dad, for example, who taught me to look for my own song, and Aunt Alta, who taught me to look for meaning here and now. Could those lessons be part of the plumbline that God set down to keep my building straight and strong? I knew that there must have been other valu-able guidelines along the way, but many of them had slipped out of my conscious mind. So I started min-ing my memories for clues to God's will.

Sometimes I just sit with eyes closed and let my mind wander back over the early years of my life. All kinds of scenes come to mind, with their sights and sounds, smells and tastes. Very often, I see that these memories carry a certain wisdom that I'd forgotten all about. For example, if I close my eyes and become very still, I can remember the night my father taught me to listen for *the song.*

I must have been about five or six. The after-noon had been one of those breathless summer scorchers during Nebraska's dust bowl years, when it almost hurt to breathe. With nightfall, a hot wind came up out of the west. Just as Mother was tucking me into bed in the back bedroom, a faint streak of lightning needled its way through the black sky between my green-and-white chintz curtains. Then came a long, low growl of distant thunder. When Mother turned out the light, there was something in the air—an invisible monster, maybe—that seemed to be closing in on me. I tried to prolong my list of God blesses, to keep her with me as long as possible, but finally she said "Enough!" and tiptoed out, closing the door behind her. Even though it was stuffy in the room, I pulled the crazy quilt up around my throat and hugged my pillow as the storm got angrier and angrier. The venetian blinds rattled, elm branches slapped against the wood siding, and the wind moaned through the cracks between the windows and sills, like a wailing ghost.

Then the whole room lit up in a fiery flash, and an instant later the sky broke open and a noise like a thousand firecrackers blasted against the roof. I wanted to get up and run to my parents' bedroom, but I was too scared to move. All I could do was scream.

The next instant, Daddy was there sitting on the edge of my bed, rocking me back and forth in his arms. As I started to calm down, he said, "Listen, Punk! Listen! There's a *song* in the storm! Can you hear it?"

I stopped sobbing and listened. Another piercing flash. Another crack of thunder. "Just listen to those drums!" said my father. "What would music be without drums? No rhythm, no depth, no spirit! What marvelous drums we have tonight!" As I listened to the drums, my clinging must have loosened a little because Daddy laid me back on the pillow. But then came the ghostly howl of the wind through the windows again, and I grabbed my dad's arm, pulling him back to me.

"Say, Punk!" he said. "I think we've got a harmonica in our band! Listen!"

I listened very carefully. Then I said, "No, I think it's a mouth harp!"

Daddy chuckled and patted my cheek. "Now you've got the idea! Just close your eyes and listen very carefully to that mouth harp. See if you can climb onto its sound and *ride on it.* You may be surprised where it will take you. But you have to keep listening!"

So I closed my eyes and listened very, very hard, and I rode on the sound of the mouth harp, all the way into the morning.

A scary storm and a caring father had shown me a way to conquer fear. Once I'd gotten in touch with that memory, I realized I could bring its wisdom into my adult life. Shortly after that, I was sitting on the stage of a very big auditorium in Omaha, about to get up to give a speech to the largest audience I'd ever faced. My heart was pounding like jungle drums. Suddenly I seemed to hear my dad saying to that frightened little girl, "What marvelous drums we have tonight!" And I smiled inside, remembering that without drums, music wouldn't have any rhythm or depth . . . or spirit!

I discovered that it's okay to be afraid, as long as you're not afraid of your fear!

Another time, on a winter night when my teenage son John was late getting home and I started worrying that he'd had a car accident, I noticed the moan of the wind in the fireplace flue. It sounded like a flute. Again, I remembered my father's advice to listen for the song in the storm. So I closed my eyes, climbed onto the sound, and rode it until John got home. I've found that it's possible to mentally ride on any sound, and that the riding will carry me through to the other side of the fear!

Mining the childhood memory of that thunderstorm gave me a tool for living—a way to face my fears instead of denying or running from them. Now, when I'm frightened by noises on a night when I'm home alone, or when I'm just simply uneasy about a difficult phone call I have to make, I try to remember that I can move beyond my fear by listening for the song in the storm. And you know, I've found that there *always is* one!

Clearly, it is God's will that I face and overcome my fears. He has "not given us the spirit of fear; but of power, and of love, and of a sound mind" (2 Timothy 1:7). I will listen for the song in the storm, and ride out my fears.

Symbolic Meaning in Everyday Events

God has always used commonplace things as symbols to make His will known to His people. Both the Old and the New Testaments are filled with individuals who saw that the ordinary signified more than itself: Adam and Eve and the tree in the garden, Noah and the olive branch, the Israelites and the pillar-shaped cloud, the Wise Men and the star. The very best example of this is Jesus, who used such ordinary things as fishing nets, lost sheep, coins, seeds, torn cloth, a loaf of bread, a glass of wine to show us transcendent meaning.

If we scratch beneath the surface of ordinary things, often we can find a lesson that reveals something that God wants us to know about His will. "We can learn our way only by taking seriously the sign that we see and the small voice that we hear."[2]

Last spring, I went through a time of really feeling put-upon. There were so many demands on my time that I felt like a piece of taffy being pulled in ten directions at once. What I really wanted to do was to spend more time working on my professional life, which demands quiet and solitude. I had to get my thoughts together for an assignment, but my calendar was full of speaking engagements, there were extra altar guild duties because of the approach of Holy Week, several people were calling me frequently for special prayers, and my family seemed to be demanding more and more attention. I was beginning to resent all these demands on my time and energy.

On top of all this, my son Paul and his family came to visit for a few days. Partly to get out of the house and away from all the confusion, I offered to take my oldest grandson, Matt, out to fly his new kite.

The wind was just right. Matt ran along, pulling

on the string, as I followed, holding up the kite, until
the wind took over. As his kite ascended higher and
higher, Matt asked, "Grandma, what holds the kite
up?"

Without thinking, I said, "The wind and the
string."

Matt, always a step ahead of his grandmother,
said, "No, Grandma. The string holds it down."

At that moment, the roll of string slipped out of
Matt's hand. And guess what happened? Of course,
the kite started to fall. So Matt and I were both right.
The same string that holds the kite down, also helps
it to rise!

That night, when I finally managed to get off by
myself, I thought about that whole episode and realized that it contained just exactly the message I
needed to hear at that busy time. Could it be that
those things I'd been thinking of as holding me down
were actually holding me up? I thought of how the
wind had taken over for me when Matt pulled on the
string. Perhaps when I try to be a servant to others,
there is a point at which I can let go and the Holy
Spirit will take over and provide the lift.

I knew then that there were certain things I
could completely release to Him at that point. But I
also knew that the other demands on my time were
strings that could give lift to my spirit. The kite was
a symbol shot through with significance for me at
that time.

I came to understand the hidden message. It is
God's will that I serve those He sends me. The Holy
Spirit will provide the lift and take over when it's
time for me to let go.

Was It Really a Coincidence?

When I pay attention to the hidden messages in everyday things, a startling thing often happens. The same message comes to me from several directions, in different ways, at approximately the same time. A good teacher repeats the important points in a lecture, and our Lord is a supremely good teacher, so He often speaks His message several times, to make sure I hear it. I used to think it was coincidence, but when it happened time and time again, I began to realize that the whole scene was being directed by my heavenly Father.

Only a few days after the kite-flying episode, I boarded an airplane for a flight to North Dakota, where I was scheduled to lead a retreat. I still hadn't been able to complete my working assignment, and despite the lesson of the kite, I was feeling frustrated about that. There was a powerful north wind that day, and as the airplane taxied onto the runway, facing north, I recalled one of the first things I'd learned when I took flying lessons years ago: *Aim the nose of the plane into the wind for takeoff.* A head wind increases the airflow across the surfaces of the wings and lifts a plane quickly. There was the same message again—*the things that seem to be holding you back are really helping you to lift off!*

As if that weren't "coincidence" enough, on the last night of the retreat, the opening devotional was taken from Mark 6:45–51, where Jesus sent His disci-

ples in a boat across the Sea of Galilee, while He
stayed behind to pray. After the men had been row-
ing for hours, unable to get anywhere at all, Jesus
"saw the disciples straining at the oars, because *the
wind was against them.* About the fourth watch of the
night he went out to them, walking on the lake."
(Mark 6:48 NIV, italics mine). The speaker concluded
her devotions with this statement: "When you find
yourself wishing for an easier life, remember that it's
when the wind is against you that Jesus comes into
your boat."

I sat there with my mouth open. I could hardly
believe it! A kite, an airplane, and a boat. Three different incidents involving the wind, three different
symbols, but one message. A lesson I needed, at the
time I needed it, each symbol adding something more
to my understanding of its truth. Who can explain it?

I'm sure it's happened to you, too. The Scripture
passage for the day or the sermon or the daily devotional seems meant just for you. Or you pick up a
book, open it at random, and find the exact words
you need to comfort a friend. Or the same Bible
passage comes to you three times in one week—in
church, in a book you're reading, and in a phone
conversation with a friend.

I don't believe it is chance. In fact, I wouldn't be
a bit surprised to find, when all is revealed someday,
that there is no such thing as a coincidence, that our
Lord uses these startling incidents to get our attention, or to tell us something very significant, or to
reveal parts of His will to us. I need to be alert for
these seeming coincidences because they are evidence of the creative hand of God operating in my
life! Now *that's exciting!*

When I got back from North Dakota, things quieted down a bit and I found time to work. I was amazed to find that ideas just started streaming in and that the finished work took a slightly different direction from what I'd planned. I seemed led to include some things that were not part of my original design and to leave out others, to the very great overall improvement of the final product. Oh *yes,* Aunt Alta. This moment *is* as meaningful as any moment in all eternity!

When I experience events that seem to be coincidences, I consider them as evidence that God is working creatively behind the scenes in some phase of my life. "Lo, these are but the outskirts of his ways; and how small a whisper do we hear of him! But the thunder of his power who can understand?" (Job 26:14 RSV).

Serendipity: Unexpected Blessings

In 1754 Horace Walpole coined the word *serendipity.* He based it on a Persian fairy tale about the three princes of Serendip (an ancient name for Ceylon) who traveled in search of treasure but rarely found what they were looking for. Instead, they kept happening onto things that turned out to be even greater treasures than those they were seeking. Although their goals eluded them, they were richly rewarded with exciting discoveries along the way. Eventually they realized that they were being guided by an unseen power that knew better than they did what was best for them. Walpole himself found that, when he learned to "dip into life with serenity" *(seren-dip)*, each day resulted in thrilling, unexpected experiences.[3]

History and particularly the world of science are stippled with examples of seemingly hopeless or failed experiments that took a surprising turn and worked out. Christopher Columbus set sail from Spain in search of a short route to Cathay, but never reached his goal. Instead, he opened the gateway to a new continent. Bacteriologist Alexander Fleming noticed one day that one of the mold spores he was studying had "spoiled." He was about to throw it away when he saw that the culture of pus-producing bacteria dissolved when in contact with the mold. Fleming's unexpected discovery led to the development of penicillin and a whole new array of life-saving antibiotics. Millions of lives have been spared because one man looked beyond the appearances of a failed experiment.

How often in my life I've felt the slap of failure . . . and how often, thanks be to God, I've known those failures to lead to unexpected blessings. As I've mentioned, I started college with the intention of becoming the world's greatest actress. If I hadn't failed at that, I wouldn't have become a speech pathologist. If I hadn't failed to get the speech therapy job I wanted in Fremont, Nebraska, I wouldn't have come to Kearney. If I hadn't come to Kearney, I wouldn't have fallen in love with a tall young architect named Rex Helleberg. If . . . the chain of events goes on, and I must eventually conclude that in life there are no missing links, that nothing is irrelevant, that there is meaning and purpose in every event, and especially in those unexpected blessings known as serendipities.

So now, when something that seems like failure comes my way, I've resolved that I will examine it expectantly for evidence of God's will in action. I will mentally pick it up, look it over, see if it points to something beyond itself. Then I'll look it over again, never throwing away my failures without asking if there could be a miracle in what seemed to be a hopeless situation. A friend of mine confided to me that her son, in a fit of anger, had thrown a treasured cup of hers against the wall, shattering it. "At first I was devastated by his action," said my friend, "but now I'm actually *thankful* that it happened, because it was that incident that got us into the family counseling that we so desperately needed."

At one time or another, we all encounter failure. When it happens to you, look closer. Examine it. Maybe you'll discover something new and good and useful in it. If the value of the experience isn't obvious right away, just trust that it *will* become apparent later.

Multiplying Your Blessings

I have come to believe that *no right action ever goes unrewarded, even though the reward may not be evident in the visible world.* The longer I live, the more evidence I see of the truth of this statement.

We had a rather startling example of it happen in our family recently. Our daughter and her husband were having a yard sale. Karen received a $20.00 bill from a woman for an old chair and a sackful of "treasures." Immediately after that, Dave made a $3.50 sale. The man handed him $4.00 and received fifty cents in change. But as Dave was clipping the money together, he noticed the $20.00 bill and thought, "Oh, no! That man gave me a twenty by mistake, thinking it was a one!" So he ran out to the man's car and gave him the $20.00. The man looked rather surprised but accepted the money and drove off. Then Karen said, "What happened to the twenty-dollar bill that woman gave me?" Of course, it was gone.

When they realized what had happened, they were aghast. The kids are just starting out and they really *needed* that $20.00. After several minutes of groaning and blaming each other, they decided that since Dave had tried to do the right thing, it would *have* to turn out right. For a while, they thought the man's conscience would bother him and he'd bring the money back, but it didn't happen. Then Karen said, "Well, I guess we'll just have to assume that maybe he needed the money more than we do."

But Dave said, "No. He was driving a Mercedes and he put the twenty in with a wad of bills you wouldn't believe!" So that wasn't it, either.

Then about mid-morning, Dave suddenly smiled and said, "You know, I just remembered something my Grandma told me once, when I lost my dime allowance. She said, "Just bless it and let it go. It'll bounce a blessing back to you!" So that's what Karen and Dave did about the $20.00 bill. Finally, after all of their if-onlys, they were able to release it and enjoy the rest of the day. They both felt good about the whole thing.

At the end of the day, they came to our house and totaled up their day's sales, which they'd written down in a notebook. Then they counted the money. They came out exactly $20.50 long! Now, that could be explained in several different ways. Maybe they forgot to write down some of their sales. Maybe the man really did give Dave a twenty. God's ways are mysterious and we may never know exactly why it came out that way. But that doesn't matter. The extra $20.00 (external reward) was nice, but even if that hadn't come to them, the grace of learning to let go was an even greater blessing. What matters is that Karen and Dave received a gift—a mighty tool for living that will last them for the rest of their lives.

If there's an unfair situation in your life, consider it an opportunity for *multiplying* your blessings. Bless it and let it go. It'll bounce a blessing back to you—even though it may be invisible! It's a law of God's will.

An Expectant Attitude Is a Magnet

I wonder why it is that sometimes I seem to receive many messages through my daily experiences and at other times I don't. Could it be that the messages are *always* coming, but that I'm more receptive at certain times than at others? I think that's it. It seems that when I'm really looking and listening for God's voice, all kinds of breakthrough insights come. When I go to church and the sermon is exactly the message I needed to hear, it probably isn't that God has singled out my problem as the focus for the day (although that might also be true). I think it's more likely that those are the times I am open to hearing His message, when I've laid my problem before the Lord and I'm *expecting* Him to give me guidance. When I am in a receptive state of mind, *God can take any passage, any article, any story or play or outer event and use it to speak exactly to my situation.*

This is especially clear to me when I seek God's counsel for a specific problem, by consulting my Bible. I used to think that the way to receive God's guidance through Scripture was the "lucky dip" method, in which you open the Bible at any page and read the first words your eyes fall upon. Sometimes that seemed to work for me, but often it didn't. Then I tried using my concordance or a topical Bible to zero in on what the Bible says about the general subject I'm bringing before the Lord, and that often provided answers. But now I use a daily Bible reading guide. I've found that if I prayerfully ask the Lord for guidance in a specific matter before I begin the assigned Bible reading for the day, He speaks directly to my situation, *through whatever the reading for the day happens to be!*

I've found that He says different things to me at various times, in the same passage, depending on what He knows I need to hear. In the same way, He can use a given passage to speak one thing to one person and something else to another.

This became very evident to me at a retreat in which I was leading the group in learning to pray with Scripture.[4] I gave them Acts 16:25–34, describing how Paul and Silas sang praises to the Lord while they were imprisoned in chains. After the group had spent time praying with this Scripture, we all came back and shared what we felt God had been saying to us.

One woman shared that she'd been feeling very tied down because she had to care for her invalid mother-in-law. "But as I prayed with this Scripture," she said, "I suddenly realized that *I can sing in my chains!* God reminded me that I am free because I can be lifted out of bondage by singing and praising Him! I love to play the piano and sing, but I've felt so burdened I haven't done it for a long time. I'm so grateful that the Lord showed me this way back to freedom."

Another woman was in tears as she told us that God had showed her, *from these same verses,* just how deeply imprisoned she was—a fact she'd been denying for a long time. "My husband and my parents and even my grown children have been trying to convince me to get help, but I wouldn't admit I needed it. But today I saw it so clearly in this Scripture reading. I knew I couldn't fool myself any longer. I'm going to get in touch with Alcoholics Anonymous."

I know from my own experience that if I come to the Lord in prayer, expecting Him to speak His will to me about any situation through my Bible reading, He will do it!

Speaking of having an expectant attitude always makes me think of my dear friend and spiritual sister, Anna. Though she's in her eighties and her health is poor, Anna's eyes sparkle, her mind is as bright as a new penny, and her outlook on life is always positive. Once, when I asked Anna her secret, she told me that every morning when she gets out of bed she says to herself, "I go to meet my good." It's Anna's way of saying *yes!* to life. When the phone or the doorbell rings or she opens a new book or goes to a meeting or to church, she says those words again. "I go to meet my good." Maybe that's why Anna has such wisdom, and why she seems always to be living close to God's will. I wouldn't be surprised if, when her time to leave the earth comes, those words will be on her lips. What a wonderful way to keep an expectant attitude.

In addition to an expectant attitude, I've found that a relaxed, receptive, inwardly confident state of mind seems to go along with those periods in my life when God speaks to me most clearly through everyday events. I need to be able to "dip with serenity," so anything I can do to get in accord with life's rhythm makes me more receptive to His messages. This includes such things as ordering my patterns of activity and rest, taking time daily for quiet prayer and meditation, and keeping myself as healthy as possible. It's all part of opening myself to receive God's best for me today.

Most important of all, I think, is to cultivate the

belief that everything is under the guidance of a loving Father, that divine order is always operating in the universe, and that this moment truly *is* as meaningful as any moment in all eternity.

God's Best
in Your Work

Make your work more meaningful.

How do we call forth the wisdom, love, and energy needed to fulfill the purposes God has assigned us? How do we carry on our day-to-day work in a way that will keep us focused in God's will? The best advice I've ever received on this came from my Aunt Alta.

Though she lived in an apartment in Omaha from September through May because of her teaching job, Aunt Alta spent her summers with Grandmother Morgan in the big old family house in rural Danbury, Nebraska. For me, spending a few days with Grandmother and Aunt Alta was among the best treats of summer.

One delicious August evening, Aunt Alta and I sat in the porch swing eating little flat scalloped-edged cookies with holes in the center, and talking quietly about such things as God and love and time and eternity. I think this particular conversation must have been during my high school years, because I was making my first tentative attempts to throw my mind across that luring yet frightening chasm between childhood and responsible adulthood. I had told my aunt that I was thinking about being a teacher someday and asked her if she thought I should. Instead of answering me, she started gently asking me questions that forced me to reflect on things I'd never thought much about, such as what did I really want out of life, and why was I thinking of teaching. Finally, she said, "Well, you're the only one who can decide."

Neither of us said anything for a while, as we gently swung back and forth, listening to the sound of the crickets chirping in the darkness and the creaking of the porch swing chains. As usual, I ate all the way around my cookie, trying to get as close as possible to the hole in the center without breaking through it. Finally, I knew what I wanted to ask.

"Well, do *you* like being a teacher?"

"Some days, yes. Some days, no. You see, it matters very much what you choose to be. But once you've made that decision, all that matters is that you make your work a prayer."

I wish I had asked my aunt how to do that. I sensed that she meant more than just praying *about* one's work. Still, I don't suppose she could have put it into words. Prayer was such an integral part of her life that it was hard to tell when she was praying and when she wasn't. Perhaps it's best that she didn't give me a formula. That way, I was nudged to try to unlock the mystery for myself.

Although I'm not always able to put it into practice, I do believe that in the years since that summer night I've come closer to understanding what Aunt Alta meant. I've worked in many different capacities (speech therapist, wife and mother, Girl Scout leader, English teacher, audiologist, writer, altar guild member, and chief dog-walker, among others), and I know that no matter what kind of work I'm doing, if I'm able to make it a prayer, the yes days and the no days beat out a gentle rhythm that is part of some symphony I don't yet have ears to fully hear, and that in the final tally, it's all okay. It's all okay. It's all okay.

With All of My Inadequacies

No matter what type of work you do, if you do it with the right attitude, it can be meaningful. You don't have to be a Billy Graham or a Mother Teresa to be used by God. Here are some things you can do to make your own work a prayer.

Offer yourself, inadequacies and all, trusting that the Lord will fill in the gaps. God often calls me to do things I don't feel fully qualified to do. For example, I'm basically a shy person. Trying to converse with strangers is often difficult for me. I don't like to be in the limelight. I'd much rather be sitting in the back of the room listening than to be up in front speaking. Yet He keeps sending me out to speak to groups, to lead retreats, to interview strangers. I haven't asked for these assignments. The calls just come in, and I'll have to admit that *after* the events are over, I'm always glad I accepted the assignments. Through them, I've met some wonderful people, and most of the time I've come away with the feeling that the purpose for which God sent me into that situation has been fulfilled—not by my doing but by His. These experiences have taught me that God calls me, not because of who I am or what I can do, but because of who He is and what He can do!

There's a marvelous passage in Job 23:14 that says, "He performeth the thing that is appointed for me." To me, this means that when God assigns me a task—whether it's to cheer up a shut-in, to lead a retreat, or to help feed and clothe a hungry family—*He* works with me, from start to finish, making it possible for me to carry it out. *He* is the One who is actually doing the work, not I. What a thrilling truth! To feel this in your bones, to know that "it is God who works in you to will and to act" (Philippians 2:13 NIV), is the first step toward being successful in what He has called you to do.

Jesus' own words help me with this. He said, "It is the Father living in me who is doing his works" (John 14:10 NIV). But Jesus is God and I'm only a human being. Never mind that! Jesus went on to say, "Anyone who has faith in me will do what I have been doing. He will do *even greater things* than these, because I am going to the Father" (John 14:12 NIV, italics mine). Think of it! Jesus' Father performed miracles through Him. And now here is that same miracle-working Christ telling me that if I believe in Him, His Father will work through me!

Can I believe that? Can I really believe it when a project I've spent weeks on is turned down and a quivering little voice within me says, "Rework it and try again"? Can I believe it when I'm about to give a talk and someone tells me there are known hecklers in the audience? Can I believe it at six o'clock on Thanksgiving morning when I discover that my oven has decided to take a vacation, and I've got eighteen people coming for dinner? Can I do the floor-scrubbing and the bed-making and the tear-drying with the belief that the Father is doing them through me?

Well, I'll tell you the truth. Sometimes I can't. But I'm working on it. I've found that during those times when I *have* been able to turn my work completely over to my heavenly Father—and sometimes it's been more an act of will than an act of faith—it has seemed as if great unseen forces have teamed up with me. The day I had to cope with the hecklers, for instance, I stopped in the middle of a sentence, closed my eyes, and silently prayed, "I can't handle this, Lord. It's all yours." Immediately, some words came into my mind and I said them. Actually, I don't even think they came into my mind. They just seemed to come out of my mouth without my even thinking of what I was about to say. I couldn't tell you what they were now if I tried, but they were the right words— the only right words for that moment. Then I picked up my talk where I'd left off and there was not another word from those who had come intending to disrupt.

I believe that no obstacle of any kind can permanently block those who truly believe God has given them a purpose (and He does give that to all who ask). It doesn't matter whether that purpose is to compose a beautiful symphony or to plant a garden in a little patch of earth; to lead a great nation or to mop up after incontinent patients; to counsel the emotionally troubled or to build a towering building, brick by brick. For those who can say, trustingly, *"He performeth the thing that is appointed for me,"* all kinds of diverse elements begin to fall into line. Hurdles, barriers, and restraints that can't be pushed away or climbed over are simply worked into the pattern, and God's purposes *are* fulfilled.

I know this is true because I've tested it in my own life. Whenever I've placed my confidence in only my own abilities, when I've depended solely upon my own self-sufficiency, when I've felt I was carrying the whole load and that without me the project of the moment would surely fail, it usually does. But when I've been able to get myself out of the way and trust the Father to do the work through me, the balance is somehow gently tipped toward fulfillment.

Know That Your Work Counts

For your work to be a prayer, you need to value what you're doing. It helps to realize that *God doesn't give out busywork.* Except for evil deeds, every kind of work is important to the whole. As long as you do the task before you with diligence and honesty, you can be sure that you are contributing to the total of human welfare, even if it seems that what you're doing couldn't possibly matter. Whether you work with your hands or your head, whether you fashion ideas or things, your labor is valuable. The food we eat, the clothes we wear, our houses and schools and churches are all the products of thousands of skills and millions of hands, and not one of them is more important in God's eyes than another.

When my brother was in high school, he went out for football. Now Donal was tall but not very husky. He was also awkward and not particularly athletic, so he ended up on the scrub team. After sitting on the bench game after game, Donal decided one night that he was going to turn in his suit. "They don't need me, anyway," he said.

My dad put his arm on Donal's shoulder and said something like this: "Well, it's up to you whether you quit or keep on. But you're wrong about one thing. They *do* need you. Without the scrub team to work out with in practice, the first and second teams would never get strong enough to win games. You are every bit as important as Leo McKillip, who's out there making all the touchdowns. And never forget this: *the win is yours.*"

Donal didn't turn in his football suit. Every day after school, he went out on the practice field and worked out. He got tackled and blocked and knocked over. Sometimes he came home with a bloody nose. And on the weekends, he'd sit on the bench and cheer like crazy as the first and second teams made touchdowns and kicked field goals. McCook High School won the state championship that year, and no one was more proud than Donal. He knew that those wins were as much his as they were Leo McKillip's.

Most of us spend the greater part of our lives on the scrub team. God just doesn't cast very many hero parts. But if I can rake leaves or do some boring research knowing that *whatever work I'm doing is somehow valuable to God,* I will have made that work a prayer. It *will* count. And the win will be mine.

A news reporter once asked Mother Teresa of Calcutta if she didn't sometimes get discouraged. "After all of your work, there are still people dying on the streets," he reminded her. Her reply was, "I am not called upon to be successful. I am called to be faithful."[1] What a glorious new way of seeing that comes when one learns to let go of external reward-seeking.

Love Made Visible

When our pastor invited me to become a member of the altar guild, I was flattered, but I soon found out that it's no glory job. It's plain hard work washing the linens by hand and ironing them to perfection. There are cleaning days, when we all meet to dust and scrub and mop and polish brass. Even in the weekly setting up and clearing, there are so many little things that have to be done just so.

One day, as I was driving home after a particularly trying experience of having to change the altar setup several times to make all the details exactly right for a particular occasion, my sometimes-negative inner voice started in on me. What if all of this doesn't really matter to God after all? What if He doesn't *care* whether the prayer book sits to the right or the left of the Gospel book? What if He doesn't care if there's a gnat-sized spot on the fair linen? What if it doesn't really matter to Him whether the altar is draped in purple or in blue during Advent? Surely there are more important things to do for God in His church!

Then, just as I rounded the corner and started up Lakeview Drive, another inner voice answered back. "You're missing the whole point," I heard. "As far as you and God are concerned, all that matters is that you do whatever work He gives you, with love." Of course! All of those external things will pass, but what happens inside of me when I do my work with love will remain forever. That's what *really* matters to God.

What does it mean to work with love? Well, if I can tend my garden as if Jesus were going to eat the vegetables; if I can write that difficult letter as though I were writing it to Him; if I can set His holy table as if I were preparing for Him to come and eat with me—all my work will be an act of love that will go on forever.

My friend Dorothy made weekly eighty-mile

round trips to visit her elderly uncle during the last five years of his life, taking him home-cooked food, doing his washing, ironing, cleaning—and receiving not so much as a thank-you for it. When I remarked that that must be a terrible burden on her, Dorothy replied, "You know, there was a time when I really dreaded those trips. But now, when Uncle Vaudie's lack of appreciation makes me resentful, I just remind myself that I'm doing it for the Lord. You can't imagine how much lighter that makes the load!"

The only sure reward on this earth for our good deeds is the spiritual satisfaction of having done them. Sometimes they bring tangible blessings into our lives, but often they don't. And that's okay! If you've done something good and seem to receive nothing in return, rejoice! It means you're amassing invisible rewards! I think one of the most beautiful statements Jesus ever made was, "Lay not up for yourselves treasures upon earth, where moth and rust doth corrupt, and where thieves break through and steal: But lay up for yourselves treasures in heaven, where neither moth nor rust doth corrupt, and where thieves do not break through nor steal" (Matthew 6:19–20).

It's true that there are parts of my work I can't love, no matter how hard I try. Probably there's a certain amount of drudgery in what you do, too. But if you and I can think of these as work done for God, by our love for Him we can make even the unlovely shine. Whatever jobs you have for today, imagine that you're doing them for Jesus, and your work will truly be a prayer.

Letting Go of the Results

Author and lecturer Sylvia Hellman wrote that "work done with anxiety about results is far inferior to work done without such anxiety in the calm of self-surrender to higher destiny."[2] That's a hard one for me sometimes. As I write this, I'm preparing for house guests. For several days now, I've been cleaning, fixing up the guest room, and planning meals. Entertaining is not my best thing. I don't know why it's so difficult for me. I guess I feel a little insecure about my abilities as a hostess. I want everything to go well. I want our guests to be comfortable and to enjoy their stay. But what if I miss a cobweb and they notice it and think I'm a sloppy housekeeper? What if that new dessert recipe flops? What if we run out of things to talk about or to do and they get bored?

The truth is our guests are much more likely to enjoy their stay if I relax than if I fret and stew around. So I will just do the best I can and stop worrying about how it will all turn out. I'm sure that's what God wants me to do, in *all* my different kinds of work. Because *undue anxiety over results actually has a tendency to poison those very results.*

But how do you get rid of anxiety over results? One thing that helps me is to get quiet, close my eyes, and visualize the hoped-for outcome as having *already happened,* and then just release the whole thing. I learned that principle from my father, years ago, although I often forget to practice it.

I must have been about ten. My dad and brother and I were on a fishing trip in a backwoods area of the Rockies. We had to cross a fast-moving stream by walking on a narrow log for about ten to twelve feet, and I was afraid of falling into the icy water. Daddy told me not to look at the log or the water but to pick a spot on the other bank and just picture myself already there. "Just throw your mind across," he said, "and your feet will follow."

He was right. It worked! It also works as a method of ridding my mind of anxiety over the results of my work. I'm glad this came up just now because I need to be reminded of it. Whenever I feel uneasy about the upcoming houseguest situation, for instance, I'm going to stop, sit down and relax, and then picture my house all neat and clean, see myself moving easily through the meals and entertaining in a relaxed way, enjoying the company. I know from past experience that if I do this, I'll be able to let go of my anxiety and things will run smoothly.

If you have a work project that is causing you anxiety, you might try my dad's suggestion. Throw your mind across and your feet will follow!

He Steers When You Move

Have you ever tried to turn the steering wheel of a parked car? Most of the newer cars have wheels that lock in place when the ignition key is removed, but even the older ones that don't have this feature are very hard to turn unless the car is moving. If you've prayed for guidance in your work but you still don't know which way to turn, maybe it's because God has a hard time steering you when you're not moving. We are to be "doers of the word, and not hearers only," the Apostle James told us (1:22). Maybe God wants to see that you're ready to get busy. If you're waiting for guidance in your work, take some kind of action, and He will steer you.

Recently, an artist friend told me that his pastor had asked him to do an oil painting for the church fellowship hall. "I really feel this is something God wants me to do," he said, "but I can't decide what to paint. I keep praying about it but I don't seem to get any direction."

I suggested that maybe he could look through some books of religious art to get a feel for what he might want to do, or reread some of his favorite Bible stories to see what mental pictures they evoked for him, and then try out a few sketches. That seemed to get him unstuck, and he finally came up with a creative painting of the disciples bringing in their nets loaded with fish. Actually, it wouldn't have mattered what he did, as long as he *took some kind of action*. It's kind of like priming the pump.

Individuals in the Bible used this as one way of discerning God's will. For instance, when Abraham asked his servant to find a wife for his son Isaac, the servant started out on his journey not knowing who she would be or exactly where he would find her, but trusting the Lord to guide him to the right young woman. The Lord did just that, and when the servant found Rebekah, he knew she was the one. "Blessed be the Lord God of my master Abraham," he said; *"I being in the way,* the Lord led me to the house of my master's brethren" (Genesis 24:27, italics mine).

After Jesus' death and resurrection, the disciples started out to spread the Good News. Only after they were on the move did God give them their directions. It was the same with Paul. After his conversion on the road to Damascus, the Lord spoke to him and he answered: " 'What shall I do, Lord?' And the Lord said unto me, 'Rise, and go into Damascus, and there you will be told all that is appointed for you to do' " (Acts 22:10 RSV). Perhaps our Lord wanted to know that Paul would obey, that he would trust enough to start out without knowing exactly what God was going to ask of him. Maybe God wants to know that about you and me, too. Later, as Paul traveled among the gentiles, teaching them about Jesus Christ, he didn't demand an advance itinerary. He just kept moving, and the Holy Spirit led him. In this way, God's plan for his life was fulfilled.

So if you're undecided about the direction God wants you to take in your work, start moving. Take some kind of action—any kind of positive action. It will unstick your steering wheel so that the Holy Spirit can begin to move you in the way God has planned for you.

But Sometimes I Fail

What if we fail? It's true that failure is *sometimes* an

indication that what we're doing is not what God intended for us to do. But if you've prayed for direction and feel that He has led you into a particular type of work, then failure may be just grist for the mill, the prod to keep you trying to do better, the goad to cause you to lift your sights.

I'm convinced that there are many people who have the ability to become successful writers but who have given up after the first couple of rejections. In fact, I believe that the biggest difference between those who succeed in writing and those who don't is not so much talent but a stubborn refusal to let rejection slips destroy them. It's the same in any line of work. Those who succeed are those who believe God has given them a purpose and who refuse to give up until that purpose is accomplished.

Here's the discouraging record of someone you've heard about since your grade school days.

1832—Lost job.
1832—Defeated for legislature.
1833—Failed in business.
1834—Elected to legislature.
1835—Sweetheart died.
1836—Had nervous breakdown.
1838—Defeated for Speaker of the House.
1843—Defeated for nomination for Congress.
1846—Elected to Congress.
1848—Lost renomination.
1849—Rejected for land officer.
1854—Defeated for Senate.
1856—Defeated for nomination for Vice-President.
1858—Again defeated for Senate.
1860—Elected President of the United States.[3]

Abraham Lincoln believed that God had given him a purpose, and he kept pushing on, even in the face of repeated failures.

A few years ago, I interviewed a crusty old Nebraska farmer who had barely eked his way through the blistering dust bowl years of the Great Depression. Time and time again, his crops failed for lack of rainfall. At other times, when there had been enough rain to give his wheat a good start, hoards of grasshoppers came in the middle of the night and leveled his crop to the ground. During many of those years, the man's wife had to take in washing and ironing to keep the family afloat. But never once did Charlie consider giving up. Come spring, he was always out there again, plowing, planting, and praying. When I asked him how he held on through all of those hardships, he said, "Well, I'll tell ya what, ma'am. You just grab ahold of failure by the tail—like a squealin' pig, y'see—and you don't turn loose of her till she gives you a gift."

When I pressed him further, he chewed on his cigar for a bit and then explained his philosophy. If you look hard enough, he reasoned, there's always something in every failure that you can use. "Maybe it's a little bit of know-how that ya didn't have before," he explained. "Or maybe that failure gave ya more time to spend with the Missus and the kids, so's you got to know 'em better. Or could be that somethin' deep down inside of ya grew a little bit by findin' out you could make it through a tight spot."

Now, every time I fail at something (and I do quite often), that picture of farmer Charlie grabbing the tail of a squealing pig comes to mind and I laugh. And after I've laughed, I look again at my defeat, and

I see that Charlie was right. Failure always comes
bearing a gift. Next time you fail at something, grab
your failure by the tail and refuse to let go till you've
discovered what gift it has brought you. Then hang
onto that gift and let the rest go.

Each day before I begin my work, I say a special
prayer. Maybe praying it could help you to find more
meaning in your work, too.

Heavenly Father, I offer myself, inadequacies and all, trust-
ing You to fill in the gaps. I believe that my work counts, no
matter how menial it may seem. Help me to labor with love in
my heart and then to let go of the results. I'll keep moving so that
You can steer me, Lord, and I'll look for the hidden gift in every
failure. Help me, Holy Spirit, to make my work a prayer this
day. Amen.

God's Best Means Living Creatively

Love is the most important ingredient.

Up until about two years ago, Christmas-eager kids had always pressured me into putting the tree up early—which meant it was usually browning and dropping its needles by Christmas. We'd go all over town trying to find just the right tree—tall, straight trunk, full branches, dark green. Then we'd bring it home and transform it into a hodgepodge, with scratched and nicked ornaments of every size and shape, strings of popcorn draped in awkward lines, red and green construction paper chains, school-made aluminum foil stars, lights of every color, and great blobs of tinsel here and there. When we were done, we'd all stand back to admire our work and—it

never failed—someone would say, "It's the most
beautiful tree we've ever had, don't you think?' And
we'd all laugh, because those words had become a
Helleberg family ritual.

But, you know what? It was true. It really was
the most beautiful, the loveliest tree yet. I think it
was because each Christmas we had more memories
of other Christmases, of earlier trees and happy,
loving times spent together decorating them. So the
words became magic. It seemed that the minute
they were voiced, Christmas really began at our
house.

But it was different a couple of years ago. For
the first time in about twenty-five Christmases, I
trimmed the tree by myself. Ever since the kids were
little, I'd looked forward to the day when I wouldn't
have all of this "help." *Then,* I thought, *I'll be able to
fix up a truly artistic tree!* And finally the time came.
Karen and Paul had both married, and John was
much too grown up at sixteen to get excited about
such a childish thing as trimming a tree. (By the time
he's twenty, he'll have outgrown his fierce sophisti-
cation. I've seen it happen with the other two. Then
he can be childlike again, without shame!)

Anyway, that year I saw my chance and seized
it. I bought the tree early to get a good pick, but I kept
it in a bucket of water until Christmas Eve. Then I
brought it into the living room and decorated it very
tastefully, with gold satin balls and red satin ribbons,
placed with an eye for symmetry and balance. Tinsel
was carefully draped, with restraint and delicacy. I
bought new lights, the tiny-bulb kind, all white,
making the tree look snow-glistened.

Then I stood back and admired my work. The tree was beautiful. It really was. But there was a gnawing emptiness in my chest. I unplugged the lights and went to bed, quietly weeping for the children time had stolen away from me, and for the magic that had flown with the years. After the holidays, I boxed up the gold balls and the red satin ribbons and the new miniature lights and took them to Goodwill.

And the next year, I got out all the old ornaments and the old lights and enlisted the help of my grandchildren. The tree we picked was tall and straight, but not nearly as perfect as the previous year's. And our decorating was not nearly as artistic. In fact, you might even say it was a bit of a hodgepodge. But when we finished trimming it, plugged it in, and turned off the room lights, four-year-old Joshua said, "Oh, Grandma! It's the most beautiful Christmas tree in the whole world, isn't it!"

"Oh yes, my little Joshie. It is. I'm absolutely sure of it."

And so magic came back to the house again.

I should have known it all along. It wasn't the straightness of the trunk or the fullness of the branches, it wasn't the placement and color of the ornaments and lights that made the tree a thing of beauty. It was the caring and sharing that came with it, the love that went into those school-made ornaments, and the rituals that were performed with such a precious sense of family oneness. These were the things that made the magic happen. *Love* was the element that transformed our imperfect hodgepodge into something beautiful.

An Everyday Act

From the moment that our Creator first spoke the universe into being, through all the ages since, *the inspired act has always been the one that is done with the greatest amount of love.* This is true not only for great artists and composers, but also for you and me in our everyday lives. In fact, an act performed with love can actually be quite imperfect and still be a thing of beauty.

Working with love we can produce masterpieces. That's true whether the result is a poem or a birthday cake, an architectural rendering or a superbly crafted chair, a back rub or a paint job on a Model A. Artists and composers and writers do not own the streams from which profound inspiration flows. They only know how to dip from them and bring back refreshment to share. Creativity can become a meaningful dimension in anybody's life. In fact, I believe that every single one of us is called to be a co-creator with God, in His ongoing act of creation. It's part of the fearful responsibility of being made in His image.

Recently, we were houseguests in the home of some friends in another state. Our hostess is truly a gourmet cook. Every evening we had dinner by candlelight, fresh flowers on the table, and unusual, delicious dishes, each one seasoned to perfection with herbs from our hostess' own garden. When I asked her how she became such a fine cook, she told me that her husband is on a salt-free diet and her daughter is a vegetarian. "I could see that either we'd have to settle for bland, uninteresting meals," she said, "or I'd have to come up with some new ways to make our dinners enticing. I found out that I really enjoyed trying out new ways to cook, finding new recipes, and surprising my family! I guess you could say that, for me, learning to cook creatively was a labor of love."

So there it is again—that all-important ingredient called *love,* which is, of course, a synonym for God. "God is love," St. John tells us (1 John 4:8). Surely creativity is one of the most Godlike qualities we possess. How can I pass up the opportunity to develop an ability that is so clearly *grace?* There are so many small ways in which we can live creatively each day, so that every moment may become a treasured one, and joy can be the pervading quality of our lives.

There are very definite things we can do to enrich our potential for inspired living. Certain attitudes, conditions, stages show up again and again when people do creative things. There is, in fact, a pattern that anyone can apply to achieve personal breakthroughs. It is based on the belief that inspiration is really God working through human beings. Staying in touch with His will is the best way to ensure creative growth in all areas of life.

Taking Time to Be

One attitude that fosters creativity is an insistence upon taking time to live in the present moment. We need to allow ourselves the luxury of sitting quietly and listening to the sounds around us, or simply focusing our mind and heart on whatever we're doing at the moment, without having to think of what will be happening tomorrow or an hour from now. Taking time just to *be* is the same principle that a good farmer uses when he allows a field to lie fallow for a time so that it can regain the essential nutrients that encourage new growth.

Frances G. Wickes tells of an incident that shows the importance of solitude in fostering creativity:

> I once found in a junk shop a Ming temple painting. The spirit of beauty shone through its battered surface. I took it home and sent for an oriental man who restored such treasures. . . . After several months, he brought it back. He had re-created it. I stood reverently before it, then said, "No wonder it took so long." "Not the work," he answered. "That was swift; but the vision. I go into the country. I sit all day under a tree. It does not appear inside me. I am too far away. I may go again and again. One day I see it. Then I work quickly."[1]

Allowing for fallow time may mean saying no to some of the many demands made on us, but living creatively is worth it. I've found that when I let my life get so clogged with external things that my alone-with-God time gets crowded out, my creativity loses its salt, and my life (as well as my cooking!) begins to taste bland and flat. I start having trouble communicating with John, my speaking engagements are met with polite but unenthusiastic response, and Rex says, "What's the matter? Don't you love me anymore?"

When that happens, I know it's time to throw a few things in the camper and drive to my favorite spot by Cottonmill Lake for a few hours, or a day, or to take a long, slow walk without going anywhere in particular, or even just to spend an hour listening to music in the dark. I know that these little ways of simply *being* make up the power line that keeps me plugged into my Source of creativity in every phase of my life.

Touch of the Master's Hand

Another valuable key for unlocking creativity is being willing to give up personal control so God's creative power can flow through you. One summer, at a Girl Scout camp in the Rocky Mountains, I signed up for a watercolor class. We climbed with our instructor (whose nickname was Bugs because she loved insects!) to a spot high above the camp-ground, where the view of Pikes Peak was breathtak-ing. After handing out paper, paints, brushes, and mixing pans, and giving us a few pointers, Bugs told us to paint the scene. The more I mixed and brushed, the more frustrated I became. The scene on my paper was absolutely flat. I felt completely inadequate and was about ready to give it all up, when Bugs came by. "Not bad," she said. "Not bad at all." Then she mixed a little of my paint and, with two quick strokes, outlined the mountain peak. With just that touch of a master's hand, my fumbling effort came to life, took on depth, and really began to look like the faraway snow-capped peak.

In just the same way, I need the touch of the Master's hand to make my work come to life. So often, I try too hard to control the direction, to make everything work out according to *my* plan. And when the project refuses to fall into line, I feel the most painful kind of frustration. But recently, I've learned to recognize that that frustration is a signal to let go. I'm beginning to discover that my best work happens when the piece seems to have a mind of its own. And I've found that if I'll let Him, the Master will complete the work I've tried so hard (and so unsuccessfully) to do. He will make it come to life. It all has to do with letting go, giving up personal control. The deeply philosophical writer, Johann Wolfgang von Goethe, said, "All creativity of the highest kind, every important conception, every discovery, every great thought which bears fruit, is in no one's control, and is beyond every earthly power. Such things are to be regarded as unexpected gifts from above, as pure divine products."[2]

In order to live a truly creative life, I must *know*, deep within me, that God is utterly trustworthy. It's the kind of trust Jesus asked of us when He said that whoever "will lose his life for my sake shall find it" (Matthew 16:25).

A couple of years ago, flying to Minneapolis, we encountered fog so dense that I couldn't see the wingtips, even though my window was right over them. While we circled the airport for what seemed like hours, waiting for clearance to land, I thought about the very real possibility of colliding with some other airplane that was also groping around in the same pea soup. As I sat there, praying and just a little less than terrified, the captain's voice came over the speaker. "There's nothing to worry about, ladies and gentlemen. My eyes can't see through this stuff any better than yours can, but the plane's radar system is working well, and we can trust it to bring us safely in." How freeing it was just to let go of my fears and tension, and trust completely in invisible guidance. In fact, I relaxed so deeply that I fell asleep while the plane circled another twenty minutes before landing safely.

The guidance of the Holy Spirit is in some ways similar to the action of that radar. When I acknowledge the fact that my own intelligence and talent are completely inadequate for whatever task is before me, and just let go, trusting completely in invisible guidance, God takes over.

Who, Me?

One thing that helps me with the letting go is the realization of my own utter inadequacy. Last summer, I helped lead a retreat on creative prayer. During a get-acquainted time the first evening, a woman named Opal confided to me, "I really don't know why I'm here. I'm not the least bit creative. I'm sure I won't be able to do what you're trying to teach, because I have absolutely no imagination."

I was able to assure Opal that that was okay! God doesn't choose those who are most qualified. In fact, He's much more likely to pick the *least* apt among us! Moses stuttered. How could he possibly be a leader of God's people? Abraham and Sarah were old and childless. Wouldn't you think they'd be the worst possible choice to be the parents of God's chosen people? Many of the prophets argued that they couldn't possibly do what God asked of them. The pages of history are filled with heroic people who have had club feet, hunched backs, speech impediments; who were lame, deaf, blind; who were called to do things they didn't think they could do—and who did them. Our Lord frequently does not pick the obviously qualified people to do His creative work. He's much more likely to ask you and me to do something we feel completely inadequate for. And that's one of the most important things we can know about the way God hands out assignments. Opal was surprised to find that when she offered her imagination to God, He guided her into some lovely imagery and to deep and fruitful prayer experiences.

What I need to remember is that *I don't have to feel qualified for what He asks me to do!* I only have to be obedient. I just have to do the very best I can, leaving the results totally up to Him. Because *that's* when He can take over! That's when God's own love can shine through me, making my acts truly creative. Only when I know I can't do it myself do I give Him a chance to show what *He* can do. Only through my weakness can He show His strength. This has been one of the most liberating lessons of my life.

A Very Old Pattern

At the same time I do have a very real part in the creative process. There are actions I need to take.

The more I've read about how the creative process works, the more I've realized that the pattern of creativity was described two thousand years ago. What it has taken modern writers thousands of words to say, Jesus expressed in three sentences:

> The kingdom of God is as if a man should scatter seed upon the ground [planting], and should sleep and rise night and day [waiting], and the seed should sprout and grow, he knows not how. The earth produces of itself, first the blade, then the ear, then the full grain in the ear [watching]. But when the grain is ripe, at once he puts in the sickle, because the harvest has come [reaping] (Mark 4:26–29 RSV).

Let's see what Jesus' parable about planting, waiting, watching, and reaping can tell us about the four stages of the creative process.

Planting

The first step in the creative process is to seed our minds, just as a farmer seeds his ground. Being creative involves planting ideas in our minds by saturating ourselves with as much information as we can find related to our project. This may involve trips to the library, interviewing an expert or consulting a counselor, talking to friends who have had similar experiences, mining memories to see what worked well in the past, listing pros and cons, looking through magazines, even listening to music that creates just the right mood. Sometimes it's very helpful to brainstorm with a group of people, having everyone call out possible solutions to the problem while someone writes them down. Nothing is analyzed at this stage; no idea is rejected. Just drop the seeds into your inner mind with a prayer for God's guidance, and let them be.

One thing I've found that really helps me during the planting stage is to try to get the *feel* of the creative solution I'm looking for. If, for instance, I have a human relationship problem, I often try to project my heart ahead and experience the feelings of harmony and love I hope will result when the problem is resolved. The important thing is to feed into your mind as much relevant material as you can find. You'll know when you've planted as much as your mind can absorb. For me, this stage usually ends with an I-can't-stand-this-any-longer feeling. Sometimes I get so frustrated, I want to give up the whole project. Then I know it's time to get away from it for a while.

Waiting

According to Jesus' parable, after the farmer plants his crop, he sleeps and rises "night and day." In other words, he simply returns to his daily routine, leaving the seeds in the ground to germinate. We have to do the same thing with any creative project. Once the mind and heart are thoroughly saturated with information about the subject, the conscious mind has to get out of the way so that the inner mind can work on the problem.

It's a bit like going fishing. When Rex was teaching John how to fish, they had a running argument most of the time because John couldn't leave his line alone. Over and over again, he'd reel it in to see if he might have a fish, or to check the bait, or to cast it out farther. Rex kept telling him that the only way to catch a fish is to put your line in and leave it there until you get a good bite.

That is a good description of what is happening in the waiting period of creativity. After you've cast out your line, you have to get your conscious mind to leave the project alone long enough for the bait you've put in during the planting stage to attract a good solution. One reason the conscious mind needs to let go of the situation is that it is very critical. It likes to run the show. The inner mind (what some call the subconscious), on the other hand, is shy and refuses to come out when the conscious faculty is waiting to squelch it with critical remarks such as, "That's silly," "It'll never work," "What will people think?" or "It's never been done before; it could be dangerous." If the inner mind steps out of hiding long enough to present an idea and it's immediately rejected, it's not likely to take the risk again.

Some of the things I've found helpful for getting my conscious mind out of the way while I'm fishing for creative inspiration include going for a walk, listening to music, sleeping (I have to have *some* excuse for those afternoon snoozes!), meditating, daydreaming, driving, keeping a dream journal—even doing routine chores such as cleaning or ironing. Just about any activity that is unrelated to the problem or question at hand will distract your conscious mind, so that your inner mind will be able to dip into the well of God's creativity. I've learned that I can trust the process—that the perfect creative solution to the problem or question I formulated is within that well. It positively *is* there, because *all* possibilities are within God's all-knowing reservoir of truth.

Watching

One day, the farmer looks out over his fields and sees that the seed has sprouted and is growing although he doesn't know how. "The earth produces of itself, first the blade, then the ear, then the full grain in the ear." Finally, he sees that all of those long hours he's spent in the fields planting, and all of his waiting, have brought results. He knows very well that *he* didn't make the seeds sprout and grow. God did. What a thrilling realization that must be for a first-year farmer!

What a thrilling realization it can be for us, when we see that the seeds we have planted in our minds and left there for God to act upon have come together in new ways, have sprouted surprising answers, have grown into fresh new forms! At some point, seemingly from out of nowhere and often very suddenly, the answer we've been seeking breaks through, flashing into our conscious mind. This is very likely to happen while we're doing some completely unrelated task. I'm sure you've had the experience of trying to remember someone's name that seems to be "just on the tip of your tongue." No matter how hard your conscious mind tries, the name won't come. Then, while you're driving to work the next day, maybe listening to the radio or humming a tune, suddenly the name pops into your mind. It's the same process! Whether it's a religious illumination, a mathematical solution, a scientific understanding, a melody for a new song, a business innovation, or an idea for the perfect gift for your spouse, it's usually accompanied by an "aha!" feeling. The phrase "like a flash of lightning" occurs again and again in descriptions of this moment of sudden knowing.

Elizabeth O'Connor calls creativity "the work of co-creation." Here's the way she describes the breakthrough moment:

> One day the cloud begins to part, pieces fit together, ideas and thoughts pour in from another realm and we know that the work of creation has been going on at two levels in us. Finally we have a piece of sculpture, a story, a building that has something more in it than all the conscious labor of our days.[3]

In addition to those breakthroughs that come during some waking activity, there are many instances in which the moment of *seeing* comes during sleep, in a dream. Robert Louis Stevenson said that many of his stories were created for him by what he called his "Little People" while he slept.[4]

Reaping

Once the crop is ripe and ready for harvesting, the farmer has to get to work on it again. "When the grain is ripe, at once he puts in the sickle, because the harvest has come." You and I have to do that, too, when we're looking for a creative answer. After we planted our seeds, we got our conscious mind out of the way so that God could work through our inner mind. New plants grew up in the form of fresh ideas. Now it's time for our conscious mind to get back into the act, which means that in one sense the show is all up to us now. We have to hold the new ideas up to the yardstick of reason. Chemical formulas glimpsed in a dream need to be verified in the laboratory. The inspiration for a poem must be translated into words on a page. The insight about how to resolve that difficult problem in human relationships needs to be acted upon. For Robert Louis Stevenson, the work of harvesting came when he used his editing talents to polish the stories presented to him in his dreams, by his "Little People." The merchant whose creative inspiration provides him with a more efficient way to run his business has to call a meeting of the employees, outline his plan, and assign duties.

Creativity is one of life's greatest delights, a spirit-lifter of the first order! One of the best antidotes I've ever found for those vague feelings of depression that sneak up on all of us at times is to turn *whatever* is on my agenda for the day into a creative project. It's always possible, no matter what has to be done, even if it's just figuring out a way to add a special dash to the salad, or to spark up an otherwise boring class lecture, or to create an eye-catching display on my office wall. If you want more insight on how to develop your creativity, please refer to the "Suggestions for Further Reading" at the end of the book.

Creative Process in Human Relationships

Creativity is a tremendous asset in all aspects of human relationships. It is especially helpful in resolving stubborn family problems. Our son Paul and his family recently spent a week visiting in our home while he was on vacation from his job. There has always been a special closeness between this tall blond son and his mother, but there have also been occasional hurt feelings over the years. I think that happens in every close relationship. For some reason, during the recent visit, Paul and I had been having a running disagreement. Each time we tried to talk it through, we ended up repeating the same old arguments, resorting to the same bristling defenses, and getting nothing resolved.

One night near the end of their stay with us, as I was having my evening prayer time, I decided to apply the stages of the creative process to this problem. To plant the right seeds, I knew I needed to pin down what I was after, as clearly and specifically as I could, so I wrote out this prayer in my journal:

> After lunch tomorrow, Lord, I'm going to sit down with Paul and talk about this problem. Please help me to hear what he's saying behind the words he speaks. Help me to see into his heart and to understand what he's feeling. Help me to be honest and clear when I tell him how I feel. Help me to risk being vulnerable. Help us, Lord, to resolve our differences in this matter, without getting angry, and in a way that will leave us both feeling good about ourselves and one another.

As I prayed I tried to mentally project ahead and plant in myself the good feelings I'd have if Paul and I could resolve our problem. I'd had a tightness in my chest all during their visit, so I tried to get the *feel* of releasing the tension in that area of my body.

Then, to get my mind off the problem and give the seeds a chance to grow, I played with my grandchildren for a while, took a walk, and went to bed early.

The next afternoon, when Paul and I sat down together, our talk started with the usual list of grievances from Paul. Some of them were valid, and I'd apologized over and over for them, but he couldn't seem to let them go. As he talked, I felt the tightness building up in my chest again.

When it was my turn I started with my usual defense, "Paul, I know I've made mistakes, and I'm sorry! What more do you want from me?"

So far, the conversation was nothing but a rerun of many others. But as soon as I'd said that, I noticed the faintest hint of redness coming into Paul's eyes. Suddenly, on an impulse that was so powerful it swept over me, I walked over to his chair, put my arms around my son, and said, "You just want to know you're loved. That's it, isn't it, honey?"

His body stiffened in my arms and he began to tremble. Finally he broke into great body-shaking sobs. "I love you, Paul. I love you so much," I told him over and over as I held him close.

Eventually, between sobs, he got the words out. "But I haven't followed through on any of the commitments I've made to you. And what about the money I owe you?"

An awareness as bright as the sun flashed into my heart. Paul had been holding on to old grievances, not because he was angry with me but because he felt bad about himself. It was just a defense mechanism.

As we sat there, arms around each other, both of us crying, I was able to reassure Paul that there is absolutely no reason for him to feel bad about himself, that the financial help we've given him is free and without strings. Our parents helped us out sometimes when we were young marrieds living on a shoestring. Why shouldn't we do the same thing for our kids?

You can't imagine the wonderful difference this has made in our relationship. Finally (thanks be to God), I was able to get behind Paul's angry words and see the hurting little child within him who was crying out for reassurance, and to give him the encouragement he so desperately needed.

Could it be, I have wondered since then, that

behind *most* angry words between people who really
love one another there's a hurt child saying, "Reassure me that you love me"? Could this be true between husbands and wives, brothers and sisters,
close friends?

*Thank You, Lord, for giving me this insight. I see that it
is Your will that I look for the hurt child whenever angry words
are spoken, no matter what the age of the one who says them.
Oh Lord, help me to see with Your eyes!*

Applying the four steps that our Lord described
in His planting parable led me toward a creative reso-
lution to a difficult family problem. Maybe it will
help you with a relationship problem in your life,
too. It's such a simple thing to remember . . . planting,
waiting, watching, reaping. Watered by the gentle
rains of love, it's an unbeatable combination!

As children of God, you and I are born to be
creators—in our careers, in our families, in our recre-
ation, in our spiritual lives, in everything we do. As
we become aware of our own creativity and begin to
encourage its growth, we'll be rewarded with a rich
harvest of increased satisfaction and joy in every
phase of our lives.

8

God's Best for You in Loving

Learn to love the unlovable, forgive and be forgiven, reach out to others.

Our daughter and her husband were married a little later in life than most. Karen was in her late twenties and Dave in his early thirties, so they're eager to have a family before it's too late, but so far no luck.

When I mentioned their dilemma to a relative who had asked about Karen, he startled me by replying, "Why does she want a baby, anyway? With the threat of nuclear war hanging over our heads, drugs and alcohol flooding the schools, the teenage suicide epidemic, terrorism, men killing each other in the name of religion, who'd want to bring a kid into *this* rotten world?"

After I got over the shock of his gruff reply, I had to admit to myself that he had a point. To give birth to a child in this time of chaos is a terrible risk. What assurance is there that Karen and Dave's baby won't be sucked into the trap of alcohol or drug abuse, or be kidnapped and tortured, or annihilated someday in a nuclear holocaust? It must be a tough decision for young couples.

It must have been a tough decision that other time, too, when chaos reigned on earth and human beings had lost their way. I wonder if God had second thoughts about sending a helpless baby into such a sinful, oppressive world—a world without hope. And to think: He knew what His Son's future held. *He knew!* Yet Love risked birth.

There are so many reasons not to love. To love is to risk being betrayed, to risk having love die, to risk being wounded. Does anyone ever grow to adulthood without having at least one broken heart? There's still a tiny little sting in my chest when I think of my first love. I wouldn't be surprised if somewhere I still have that note that started out, "Dear Marilyn, It's been a wonderful year, and I hope we can always be friends, but last night, as I was out with Carolyn. . . ." That night, I told God I'd never love anyone again.

But of course I did. And there have been other rejections, other deep hurts. I believe that Rex and I have a solid marriage, but we sometimes hurt each other. Just last weekend, he wanted me to go camping with him but I said, "Sorry. I can't go. I've got deadlines to meet." Then on Sunday afternoon, a friend called and asked me to go to an art exhibit with her, and I dropped everything and went. I didn't even realize I'd hurt my husband until he left for work Monday morning without saying good-bye. How could I have been so thoughtless? Is it possible to live together intimately without stepping on one another's heart now and then? I don't think so. And the children. Their pain is mine. I hurt when they hurt. Do you ever get over that? Sometimes I think about our Lord's mother, Mary. How could she bear to stand below the cross, watching her Son suffer and die? If she had known what pain He would bring into her life, would she have been so quick to say to the angel, some thirty years before, "Be it done unto me . . ."?

Oh yes. I think she would. The need to love is stronger than all the pain, suffering, and darkness in the world. And always, always, it is worth the risk. If there's one thing that a half-century of life has taught me about human relationships, it's this: God's best for me means saying "yes" to love.

But what does that mean, and how can I love more authentically? Is it possible to love the unlovable? Where is God's will in those everyday relationships that grind and chafe? What about "evil people"? Is there a way to break through the emotional barriers that separate us? What if I've tried to forgive and can't?

The Smallest Act

Sometimes I wish I could be a Mother Teresa or an Albert Schweitzer. Now *that's* unselfish, Christlike love at its best. Surely that's the kind of servanthood God wants from me, too. How pitifully short I fall! But over the years, our Lord has tried to teach me that although love sometimes makes itself known by great, sweeping acts of self-denial and sacrifice, more often than not, it tiptoes in on tiny bare feet.

One blustery March day in the thick of World War II, Mother and I stood on board the navy troop ship *U.S.S. Haskell* and kissed my father goodbye, as he sailed off to war. I tried to memorize the feel of his bristly cheek against mine, the scent of his shaving lotion, the tilt of his head as he winked at me . . . because I was afraid I'd never see him again. Then Mother and I turned quickly and started down the gangplank. (When you know you're about to be torn apart inside, you want to get it over with.) But we kept turning back to wave. That was when I noticed the tears running down my father's face. Suddenly embarrassed, he started to search his pockets for a handkerchief. At that moment, Mother took her own frilly little linen hanky out of her purse, ran back up the gangplank, dried Daddy's eyes with it, and tucked it into his pocket.

It was such a little thing. Silly, even. But somehow that small act of love was mightier than all the horrors of war. And in that moment, I knew that nothing could ever separate those two. Not miles, not oceans, not war, not even death.

Hidden Tears

That wasn't the only thing the war taught me about loving. Wars are terrible things, but even the worst atrocity can bring with it lessons for living.

I've always tended to hold in my painful emotions, to wear a smiling mask when I'm dying inside, to cry only when I'm sure the door is locked and no one else is home. That's why it does me good to remember, now and then, those first few weeks when Mother and I lived alone while my dad was at sea.

I was afraid that Mother would go around crying a lot once we were home. But she didn't. Instead, she erected a cold, gray wall around herself. There were no tears, no self-pity, just a rigid, distant stoicism that made me feel lost. Somehow, it became an unwritten rule that we never, never talked about Daddy. It hurt too much. Now and then I sensed an attempt by Mother to reach through her wall to touch me, and I desperately wanted to reach back, but we just couldn't seem to break that barrier.

Then one day, Mother announced that she had decided to make an Easter dress for me. We went together to pick out the pattern and the lovely blue taffeta. Both of us got really excited about the project. I helped her cut it out and watched her in the evenings as she sewed. Although we still didn't talk much, we found working together better than hiding in our rooms.

On Friday night the dress was ready for a final fitting. I tried it on and was thrilled! It looked even nicer than I'd hoped. As I paraded around in front of the full-length mirror, posing and picturing myself swishing down the aisle in church on Easter morning, I blurted out without thinking, "Oh, I wish Daddy could see me in this dress!"

I felt the silence fall. My bones picked up the chill. As I took off the dress, I heard Mother tiptoe out, go to her room, and close the door.

Never in my life had I felt so alone. In my adolescent mind, distorted by loneliness, it seemed that I'd been forsaken by my father, and now by my mother. I tried to pray but couldn't. Had God forsaken me, too?

After a while, the phone rang and I heard Mother answer it. I think she thought I was asleep, but I heard her say to her friend, "Oh, it's so hard, Audra. But I have to keep up a good front for Marilyn. I cried in front of her once, and it upset her so. I don't ever want her to see me crying again, so I spend a lot of time in my room."

I could hardly believe it! As soon as she hung up the phone, I went into the kitchen, put my arms around her, and said, "It's okay to cry, Mom. Really."

I felt her body stiffen. Then the tears came— both hers and mine. We started talking about Daddy, and all of our accumulated fears came tumbling out.

Periodically, we'd hold each other, rocking back and forth, celebrating the wonderful discovery of our need for each other.

It is our Lord's will that we share our pain. If you're hurting today, risk opening yourself to a loved one. If you know someone who is sad, let that person know, in little ways, that it's safe to let his or her pain out with you. It's the way Christ taught. "Bear ye one another's burdens, and so fulfil the law of Christ" (Galatians 6:2).

An Irrational Act

Thanks be to God, my father did come back from the war, and he and mother had many more years together. But that moment on the ship was echoed on the night he died. I've been told that as they carried him out of the house on a stretcher, Mother ran after them and covered his motionless form with the blanket from their bed, tucking it gently around his shoulders and up under his chin. Surely she knew he was already dead. A meaningless gesture, perhaps. An irrational thing to do. But that's another thing about love. It doesn't always play by the rules of logic.

What could be more irrational than to "love your enemies, bless them that curse you, do good to them that hate you, and pray for them which despitefully use you, and persecute you" (Matthew

5:44). Yet that's what Jesus asks of us. Impossible! But a few years ago, he gave me a way to make that unnatural act a little easier.

That way came to me at a time when I was having trouble coping with a neighbor who was considered a troublemaker by everyone on the block. Author and speaker Harold Hill says that everyone has a "favorite stinker,"[1] and I guess this lady was mine. She deliberately set friend against friend with remarks such as, "Don't tell Jan I told you, but you should hear what she said about the way you wear your hair." Whenever her five children started getting on her nerves, she'd send them all over to my house, without checking to see if it was convenient for me. This woman also had a habit of dropping in on me when I was busiest and refusing to take a hint. I tried to be nice to her, but inside I boiled. Then I'd feel guilty about my anger.

After one particularly annoying incident, I mentioned my frustration to a trusted spiritual advisor. "Jesus said I should love my neighbor," I said, "but how can you love someone who is so obnoxious?"

His answer was an eye-opener. "Jesus didn't say we have to love the *personality* of everyone we know. *Just love the child of God within her.*"

What a freeing insight that was! After that, when this neighbor imposed on me or gossiped about me or sent her kids over to my house uninvited, I'd admit to myself and to God that I didn't like her personality. Somehow, just admitting it took the edge off my frustration. Then I'd ask the Lord to help me see His child within her. Sometimes, as I did this,

I'd glimpse a hurt and wounded little girl within this adult woman. Her personality didn't change, but I didn't get as annoyed with her after that. Sometimes I even sensed a tiny, flickering light glowing back at me from her inner child.

Born to Be Evil?

Some think that there are certain people in the world who are just basically evil, but I don't. Sure, there are people who do evil things. But the longer I live, the more convinced I've become that, deep down, underneath all the defenses and masks and stinging bristles of self-protection, there is an image of the Creator within even the most violent criminal. I don't believe that there are any hopelessly evil people—only desperately wounded souls, whose child of God has become trapped within them.

When I was a young public school speech therapist, I worked with a twelve-year-old boy who stuttered. That wasn't Daniel's only problem. He loved to shock me by telling me about the fun he had torturing frogs, about the time he threw a mud ball in the teacher's face, and about the many fights in which he (big for his age) beat up other kids. He was once expelled for knocking another boy out by hitting him over the head with a baseball bat.

But through all this, there was one thing that

didn't quite add up. Daniel kept talking about his beautiful mother and telling me wonderful stories about how much she loved him and all the fun and happy times they had together. I knew that his parents were divorced, that his father was in the penitentiary, and that he lived with his grandparents, so I couldn't figure it out.

Then one day when I got to school, the faculty lounge was abuzz. Daniel had cornered two girls behind an apartment building, pulled a knife on them, and forced them to undress. One after another, the teachers expressed their hopelessness.

"Well, he's just a no-good kid. What can you expect, with his dad in the pen? It's just a matter of time before Daniel will be there, too."

"Bad blood, that's what it is. Bad blood."

"Well, they'll have to send him to 'the hill' [the correctional institution for boys] for sure now. Trouble is, it won't do any good. There's just no hope for him."

Fortunately for Daniel, he got a judge with a heart, who refused to label him as evil. Instead, he ordered psychological counseling and asked the social workers to step up their efforts to find a foster home for the boy.

Daniel had asked me to be there on the day of his hearing. He said he wanted me to meet his mother, but I didn't see anyone there who seemed to be filling that role. He was back in school the next day, so when he came in for his speech therapy, I asked him which woman at the hearing was his mother.

At first he just stared at me. Then he started to tremble. "She wasn't there. I wrote and asked her to come but she didn't show up. Didn't even bother to answer my letter. She doesn't care a hoot about me. All of that stuff I've been telling you about her is a lie." Then big, husky, tough Daniel put his head in his hands and began to sob. "I just pretended all of that. Nobody's ever loved me. My grandparents only took me because they had to. They can't stand me. That's why I do the things I do—to get even, I guess. All I've ever wanted is for somebody to love me."

Daniel's story has a happy ending. In a few weeks, he was taken in by a middle-aged couple whose only son had been killed in a skiing accident. It took a while before Daniel could believe anybody really could love him and want him. But when he finally learned to trust their love, he started to blossom. The last I heard, he was working as a counselor in a Christian home for troubled boys.

Thank God for the judge who refused to label Daniel as bad. Thank God for the people who saw through his woundedness and loved the child of God within him back to life. Thank God for His own Son, who never gives up on anybody. "For it pleased the Father that in him [Christ] should all fulness dwell; And, having made peace through the blood of his cross, by him to reconcile *all things* unto himself . . . whether they be things in earth, or things in heaven" (Colossians 1:19, 20, italics mine).

God's best for me means looking for the child of God in every person, especially those who are the least lovable, today and every day.

Everyday People

It may be difficult to see the image of God in those whom society has labeled as evil, but far more difficult is the task of coping, on a day-to-day basis, with the irritating behavior of those you live and work with.

Last summer, I co-directed a week-long spiritual growth retreat. The other speaker made the very good point that "your best spiritual directors are the people you live with, because every time they irritate you, they're showing you where you're stuck." It's true. I came home at the end of that week to a sinkful of dishes encrusted with the remains of canned chile, fried eggs, and Hamburger Helper. The family room carpet had a veneer of dog hair, popcorn, and crushed potato chips. The beds were a tangle of twisted sheets and quilts, and my shoes stuck to the kitchen floor with every step.

What a letdown to come home to *that*, after a wonderful week of getting closer to the Lord. After giving Rex and John a perfunctory hug and kiss, I said, "Gee, what a mess! Didn't you guys do *anything* while I was gone?"

Rather sheepishly, John opened the door to the dining room and led me in. The table was beautifully set, complete with lighted candles and fancy place mats. On the wall above the table was a banner, made with magic markers, that said, "Welcome Home, Mom! We missed you! We love you!" My two guys had a roast and baked potatoes in the oven and they'd fixed my favorite pistachio pudding.

Talk about finding out where you're stuck. Talk about a dramatic adjustment in values. How important is a little dirt and clutter, anyway, when you've got people who love you? I apologized to Rex and John for my cross words and hugged them both. We had a wonderful meal together, and as I went about the tasks of putting things back in order that evening and the next day, I kept silently singing praises to the Lord and thanking Him for the priceless gift of my family, sloppiness and all.

Still, there are those annoying habits. Rex often interrupts me in the middle of a sentence, or changes the subject at the heart of an important conversation. John turns his stereo up too loud and puts off his lawn mowing. Both of them make a lot of demands on my time. (I do plenty of things that annoy them, too, such as starting to clear the table before they've finished eating, and talking on the phone too much.) There are times when I envy Thoreau, who was free enough to go off into the woods by Walden Pond, build himself a little cabin, and commune with nature; or those who live in monasteries and hermitages, and spend their days getting closer to God. And when I'm annoyed, I tend to think how much easier it would be to lead a holy life if I lived alone. But would it? Could I practice patience with a deer or a rock? Could a cottonwood teach me how to forgive? Maybe there are some saintly people who can grow spiritually in isolation, but I think that most of us need other people, not only to keep loneliness away, but also to show us where we're stuck.

Putting up with a certain amount of friction between ourselves and those we love is just part of living. Besides, isn't it possible that that very friction, like the grinding and polishing of gem stones, may be just what's needed to smooth out our rough edges?

And this brings me back to my belief that God is in control of His world and that He really does have a plan for each life and a master blueprint for the universe. I am convinced that each person who enters my life is there for a purpose (as I am in theirs for a reason), and that all of my problems with other people, properly seen, are opportunities for growth.

I need to keep reminding myself of this truth, especially with a certain woman. We have been friends for years, and she probably knows me better than anyone else outside my family. That's just the trouble. She knows my weaknesses all too well, and when I need to be reminded of them, she is glad to do the job. She's a fine Christian woman, who seems to feel a personal responsibility for the welfare of my soul. She tells me the mistakes I'm making in raising my children, lets me know when she thinks my husband feels neglected, and points out what's wrong with my writing. There are times when the old cliché seems to fit: With friends like that, who needs enemies?

But if I can get past my first reaction—which is always defensive—to her criticisms, very often I find that what she's saying is something I really need to think seriously about. After I finish ranting and raving to Rex about her latest needling, I can begin to look at it more objectively. Even if I still think she's all wrong, the experience usually humbles me, and

God knows I need that now and then. Thanks be to God, I have other friends who are kind and support-ive and accept me as I am. But I have an idea that this friend does more for my spiritual growth. Perhaps there's someone like this in your life, too. Would it help if you tried to think of her (or him) as God's instrument for your spiritual growth? That's what the person is, you know.

The Hardest Part

By far the most difficult thing our Lord asks of us, in regard to human relationships, is to forgive. But ask it He does . . . and in no uncertain terms. "But when you are praying, first forgive anyone you are holding a grudge against, so that your Father in heaven will forgive you your sins too" (Mark 11:25 TLB). But how? You can will it, you can *say* "I forgive," but if your heart isn't in it, the resentment will still cling to you.

A couple of years ago, I asked a friend for her prayers concerning a serious problem within our family. She agreed to keep it confidential and I trusted her, but before long several people asked about the problem, which they'd heard about from the friend whose prayers I'd requested. It caused a great amount of embarrassment for me and other members of my family. I was furious! How could she do that to me? We got together and tried to talk it

out, and I said, "I forgive you," but I just couldn't
seem to let go of my resentment.

Then one night during my prayer time, I asked
the Lord to help me *truly* forgive this friend, and He
gave me a visualization that has helped me many
times. In my mind's eye, I saw myself in the church
of my childhood. It was nighttime, and as I walked
in I saw Jesus standing near the altar. He was the
transfigured Christ, and light was beaming out from
His glowing body. As I walked toward Him, I realized that I was carrying an unlighted candle. When
I held my candle up to His light, it was ignited, and
as I watched, the light of His love traveled down my
arm, across my chest, and into my heart. Oh, how
warm and wonderful it felt! Then, in my imagination, I turned around and saw my friend standing
there in the church with me. She was holding something up to me. It was an unlighted candle! With just
a little bit of reluctance, I reached toward her candle
and saw the light of Christ's love pass from mine to
hers. Then it traveled down her arm and into her
heart, forming an arc of light between us that bonded
us in His love. I just held onto that warm, almost
electric, connection for a few moments and then let
go, with a prayer of thanksgiving. I repeated the
visualization every night during my prayer time,
until that bonding became so real that I knew I had
truly forgiven my friend.

Since then, I've been using that visualization
prayer whenever I need to forgive someone or get rid
of a resentment. Maybe there's someone in your life
you've been trying unsuccessfully to forgive. Perhaps the candle-lighting prayer will help you to let
go of your grievance.

Who Needs Love, Anyway?

I think most of us are just a little bit afraid of emotional intimacy, afraid to allow ourselves to be vulnerable to another. Although we feel alone and want to reach out to those near us, not only to help them but also to break out of our own isolation, we find ourselves reaching out with one hand, while holding people at arm's length with the other.

Sometimes that's because we've lost someone very dear to us, and we don't ever want to face that kind of pain again. But there *is* a way through.

Rex's sister and her husband were killed in a Christmas night car accident in 1968. A few days later, their fourteen-year-old son, who was home alone at the time of the accident, came to live with us.

If Tom had been a few years younger the night he came to us, shivering from the January cold and clinging to his black dog, I could have put my arms around him and said, "Go ahead and cry, honey. Let it all out." It would have been easier that way. But instead he was dry-eyed and his grief was tightly locked up somewhere inside him.

The mother in me grieved for the part of him that was still a child as I watched Rex carry in the few belongings that were all Tom had left of his parents. Oh, how I wanted to mother him and love him back to wholeness! But it soon became very clear that Tom wanted no part of that.

He seemed to face his devastating loss with

courage and manliness. For the first two weeks, he
acted like a guest in an atmosphere of strained polite-
ness and overconcern. It wasn't long, however, before he was "flying" John (then eight months old)
around the house and laughing and joking and, yes,
fighting with the older children. He seemed to adjust
quickly to the new school. Yet somehow, though he
lived in our house, I knew that it wasn't really *home*
to Tom.

And I knew that there were times when the
sealed wound ached within him: when we made a
trip to Lincoln and stopped to check the empty
house; when one of our children brought out an old
family picture of Tom on his mother's lap; when he
was elected to the student council at school and
someone said, "Your mother would have been so
proud of you." At these times especially I wanted so
desperately to put my arms around Tom and say, "I
understand how you feel."

But I just couldn't. There seemed to be an im-
penetrable wall surrounding his hurt. Although my
head knew better, my heart felt totally rejected.
Gradually, I stopped trying so hard to break through
to Tom.

Somehow we got through the winter, with wide,
wide spaces between us. I wasn't surprised that Tom
seemed depressed and edgy after the trip to visit his
parents' graves on Memorial Day. The next day was
gray and gloomy and the children had been bickering
since morning. So I didn't think much about it when
Tom stomped out the door with his dog on a leash
after a fight with ten-year-old Paul about nothing at
all. But Karen followed him and in twenty minutes

she was back, breathless and on the verge of tears. "Mom! Tom's running away. He's on the fairgrounds road."

I put down the potato I was peeling, phoned Rex, and left the older children to watch the baby. I drove to and through the fairgrounds, then circled block after block, but Tom had disappeared. By this time, Rex was also searching in his car, so I started home to check on the children. Tears were stinging my cheeks now as I realized how much I loved this tall, quiet boy.

As I pulled into the driveway, the children came running out to meet me. Tom had come back while we were out searching.

I found him lying on his bed, scratching his dog's ears. *Oh Lord,* I prayed, *do I dare reach out to him again? Will he just turn an angry back to me or tell me to go away?* Timidly, tentatively, I walked in and sat down on the bed beside him. And I heard myself say, "I think I understand how you feel, Tom. Sometimes I have a deep, lonely ache within me, too."

Tom stopped petting his dog and looked up at me without moving. Then, in a faraway voice, he said, "You do? You?"

"Yes. And sometimes I'm afraid to let anybody know I'm hurting."

He looked deep into my eyes, paused a long time, and then said, "Yeah. Me too." It wasn't much. But it was a little bridge. Then he sat up, gave his dog a brisk rubdown, and said, "I'm so glad to be home." And I realized with a sudden stab of joy that he meant right here, at our house.

I think everyone sometimes has a lonely ache

within, and that we all have *some* fear of giving ourselves, fully, in love to another. But I also know that Christ meant for us to overcome that fear, to reach through it. And here's the real point: The way to reach through is to be vulnerable to one another. *It isn't our strengths that bridge the empty spaces. It's our weaknesses that create the breakthrough bonds between us.* Maybe that's because our weakness calls forth Christ's strength. "My strength is made perfect in weakness" (2 Corinthians 12:9).

Eighteen years have passed since the day that Tom found his way home. He has been a very important part of our family ever since. He's a successful lawyer in Los Angeles now, and last spring we had the very great joy of being the family of the groom, when Tom married a lovely young physician named Patricia. Thanks be to our loving God who reaches into our brokenness and redeems it, and who gives us the courage to keep risking love.

It seems that almost every morning the newspaper brings word of another horror—a hijacking, or a terrorist attack, or a hostage situation somewhere in the world. Even the state and local news often includes a murder, a rape, or a burglary. The faces of hatred are glaring. Today I'm tempted to feel discouraged about human nature. And when I look out over the little valley behind our house, I see that everything is dying. The prairie grass is a dry gray-brown, the cottonwoods are almost stripped of their leaves, and a mournful wind whistles through the dry cornfields to the west of us and moans around our eaves. But then I notice that there are children playing out in the valley. While I've been watching, Stevie Grandon has just picked up his little sister Eva and is trudging up the hill with her. It looks as though she has a hurt foot.

Only a tiny incident of caring. In the face of all the horrors of our stricken earth, how can it matter? Yet I've come to know that coupled with God's strength, even the smallest act of love is more powerful than all the evils of our wounded world.

9

God's Best,
Even in the Darkness

*See Him in the midst of trouble and let Him help
you work through to better times.*

"I used to believe in God, but when I was twelve, my
mother got cancer of the stomach. She had always
been a faithful Christian and had taught us children
to pray from the time we could talk. I prayed and
prayed that God would let her live. I *needed* her! I'm
sure that my mother prayed too, and my brother and
my two sisters. I wouldn't be surprised if even my
dad, who never talked much about religion, also
prayed for Mom to live. But it didn't do any good.
She died anyway. I guess in a way I've been mad at
God ever since. How can you believe in a God of love
when young mothers die, and little children get run

over by cars, and tornadoes wipe out whole towns?"

These words, spoken to me by someone I love very much, are echoes of the cries of men and women throughout the centuries, raging against God for allowing such terrible pain and suffering to happen in the world. I can't blame this person for his feelings. I think they are perfectly natural. I suspect that every good Christian has, at one time or another, asked that fearful question, "Why does a loving God permit suffering?"

Suffering Is Not Punishment

Many of us grew up with the idea of a very punitive God who was sitting up in His heaven watching our every move, waiting to zap us if we misbehaved. Anything that went wrong was sent as a punishment. But that is a mistaken view, one we need to rid ourselves of. Although God is a firm and just Lord, He is, above all else, a loving and merciful Father. Jesus made that very clear in His parable of the prodigal son (Luke 15:11–32). Even though the younger son had wasted his inheritance with riotous living, when he came home penitent, his father "was filled with compassion for him; he ran to his son, threw his arms around him, and kissed him" (verse 20 NIV).

Remembering an incident from my childhood has helped me correct my own mistaken view of God as the punishing parent. The scene in my memory

seems rather idyllic at first, misty around the edges.
A soft night, kids playing, laughter, closeness, cama-
raderie. But there is something at the center of the
memory I don't want to look at. A wheelchair. A girl
named Joyce, just a few years older than I, her arms
flailing around, hands bent sharply inward at the
wrists, her mouth pulled open and downward on one
side, saliva dripping onto her bright orange blouse.

Joyce was often wheeled over into our yard by
her sister, who joined in our games. But we never got
used to it. We would play our game, each of us being
very careful not to look in Joyce's direction. Yet there
she sat, her presence needling us like a sticker in the
sole of a bare foot.

I don't think any of us kids had ever heard the
words *cerebral palsy*. So what we knew about Joyce
was that she couldn't walk, could talk only in la-
bored, yawnlike syllables, couldn't go to school. She
was different—painfully, dreadfully different. And
we knew from whispers that she was like that probably because somebody in her family had done something bad. Joyce was that somebody's secret sin made
visible, put here to be an inescapable threat to boys
and girls like us. If we weren't good, something terrible would probably happen to us, too. Joyce was
God's punishment—a God who punished people by
making bad things happen.

One autumn night, all the neighborhood kids
were in our yard talking about going back to school.
We stood around under the street light, chattering
over the top of Joyce's head as if she weren't there—
about new dresses for school, books, teachers,
friends we hadn't seen all summer. As we talked, I

caught a glimpse of Joyce's face. There were tears running down her cheeks. I looked away and kept on talking.

But that night I couldn't sleep. Whenever I closed my eyes, Joyce's tear-smeared face glowed behind my eyelids like the afterglare from looking at the sun. The possibility that she might have feelings stabbed at me. If she could hurt, then that meant that she was a real person, like me, and not just somebody's punishment come to life.

I got up out of bed, went into my parents' bedroom, and patted my mother's face until she opened her eyes. I told her I had a bad stomachache. I couldn't tell her that it was my heart that was sick. Maybe I didn't really know the difference myself. All I knew was that after that, as hard as I tried I could never fully recover my old indifference to Joyce.

I hurt that night, not because God wanted to get even with me for hurting Joyce, but because He wanted me to learn compassion. My God chastens. He does not retaliate.

Suffering Nevertheless

If suffering is not punishment from God, what causes it, then? A large part of our suffering results from our own negative thinking and wrong choices, both individually and collectively. This includes such things as wars and crime and emotional abuse. So why doesn't God stop such horrors? He could, of course, stop them all. Instead, He has given His children the weighty gift of free will. As we discussed earlier, this gift is what makes us human, even though we often abuse it. A world without this kind of pain would be a world without choice. If I were not free to choose to cheat on a Latin test, neither would I be free to choose to sing praises to God.

But there is another kind of suffering that is not (or at least not primarily) caused by human beings and includes such things as earthquakes, floods, drought, and to some extent diseases. Why does God allow these horrors? I don't know. I simply don't know. But I do believe that these things are like the dark threads in a weaving, which help to define the pattern. I also believe that if I could see the whole weaving, I'd recognize their value.

Sometimes God allows negative things to enter our lives in order to help us grow. A child who is protected from all suffering will never learn how to live effectively in the real world. Difficulties, trials, even pain and suffering help us grow and increase our strength and endurance. That is also true in the spiritual world. God wants only the best for us, and that best includes spiritual growth. God does not *cause* our suffering. "For he does not willingly bring affliction or grief to the children of men" (Lamentations 3:33 NIV). But when bad things occur, He expects us to *use* them to grow in some way. Peter wrote about those who "suffer according to the will of God" (1 Peter 4:19). But he went on to say that "after you have suffered a little while, the God of all grace, who has called you to his eternal glory in Christ, will himself restore, establish, and strengthen you" (1 Peter 5:10 RSV).

When my son John was trying to learn how to ride a bicycle, he didn't want training wheels because his friend didn't have any on his bike. So guess who became his training wheels? I'd run along beside him, holding him up, until I felt he was steady enough. Then I'd let go. This was followed by wobbling wheels, falls, and tears. There was quite a run on Band-Aids at our house for a while. In a sense, each painful fall hurt me as much as it did John. But then there came a bright June day when I let go and my son pedaled away into a brand new level of self-esteem. I could have prevented his falls. I could have saved quite a few Band-Aids and tears. But then, would John have learned to ride his bike?

That may be a rather frivolous example, but I think it makes the point that like a good earthly parent, God's best for His children includes some opportunities for growth—and growing sometimes hurts.

Looking in the Rearview Mirror

It's not always possible to see the good in a bad situation. But if we look back on our sufferings, we can often begin to see them in a new light. Once, when Rex and I were driving down a mountain pass after a summer picnic high above timberline in the

Colorado Rockies, we had not one but two flat tires. Since we'd used our spare on the first flat, we had to flag down a car, ask the driver to take the tire to a service station in Manitou Springs at the bottom of Ute Pass, and request the mechanic there to repair it and bring it back to us.

All that frustration on the highway had cancelled out the good feelings of the afternoon, and we both sat in our sidelined car grouching about the sorry state of affairs. "What did we do to deserve this?" was our constant refrain.

The service station attendant finally arrived with our repaired tire and we thanked him, paid him, and finished our descent. It wasn't until we were all the way down from the mountains that it occurred to me that I hadn't paid the least bit of attention to the beautiful scenery of the Pass, which I usually drink in with great thirst. Then I looked in the rearview mirror. There stood Pikes Peak, tall and stately, silhouetted against a turquoise sky. It had, of course, been visible all through the trip, but I'd been too caught up in the trials of the day to notice.

I need to remember to look in the rearview mirror as I travel through life. All of us need to view the road behind us from our present perspective—to see both where we've been, and also what we've missed while we were going through it. This is especially important for those situations that have brought us great pain or that have seemed unusually difficult as they were happening. It's not good to *dwell* on past suffering, but a prayerful glance over one's shoulder now and then can be very revealing. Perhaps we can see that a fearful uncertainty forced us to make a necessary decision that we'd have avoided otherwise; or that our unhappiness was a consequence of something we did that doesn't have to be repeated; or that a failure in one area led to success in another; or that the pain broke up some hardness of heart in us, preparing us like newly plowed ground for certain plantings.

Pain Can Be a Magnet

As I look back at some of the difficult times in my life, I can see that they have served as magnets to draw me closer to Christ.

One of the most unhappy times of my youth was the period during World War II when my father was in the navy and stationed in Chicago. My brother was in college, and Mother took me out of school and moved us to an apartment in the Windy City. That should have been quite an adventure for an eighth grader, but I hated it. In the first place, I had to leave behind my very first boyfriend, knowing that he'd quickly find someone else (he did). Besides that, I just didn't fit in with the sophisticated students in the Chicago school I was attending. I was excruciatingly shy, I didn't have the right kinds of clothes, and a bad case of acne made me very self-conscious about my appearance. Mother encouraged me to invite girls to the apartment after school and for dinner, and sometimes they came, but they seldom invited me to their homes. I was so lonely!

But I know now that it was during that time of loneliness that I came to know Jesus, not just as somebody who lived two thousand years ago, not as an all-powerful Being in heaven, but as my very best Friend. I'd lie in bed each night talking with Him, telling Him about all the awful things that had happened at school that day. I knew He understood. In the morning I'd complain to Him about having to go to that terrible school, and He'd agree to go with me. During recess, when the other kids were playing games and laughing and having fun, my Friend and I would sit together, leaning up against the building, silently talking over the worries I had about the war, my little triumphs (a good grade on a test or a compliment from the teacher), and some big questions, such as "What should I be when I grow up?" Well, I'm rarely ever lonely any more, but in all the years that have passed since those Chicago school days, I've never really lost that best-friend relationship with my Lord. It was a gift of my loneliness.

Like emotional anguish, physical pain can also draw us closer to Christ. For at least twenty-five years, I've had recurring migraine headaches. Unless you've experienced them, you can't really know how agonizing they are. Sometimes the pain is so bad that I have to scream out. Often I cry, "O God, help me!" but not because I expect Him to immediately relieve the pain. It just doesn't happen that way. I do it because I can't help it. But in that cry I've experienced what the Psalmist meant when he said,

"Out of the depths have I cried unto thee, O Lord" (Psalm 130:1). I've discovered that my Lord is a Being who hears that cry and answers it with His presence.

Please don't misunderstand. I'm not masochistic. I'd never go in search of pain, and I avoid it whenever possible. If God leads me to a way of preventing or curing the migraines, I'll grab it and run, with great joy and thanksgiving. It's just that when pain does come unbidden, I know that I can *use* it to come closer to Christ.

Perhaps as you look in your own rearview mirror, you'll recall some times when loneliness and pain have brought you closer to God. And perhaps the next time you are in pain, you can remember that Christ made pain and death the means to life and peace. Then you can offer your suffering to Him. When you're hurting, know in your heart *that every pain or grief offered to Christ can be taken up and used by Him in His work of overcoming evil.*

The Darkness I Create

What can we do, however, with suffering that is brought on by our own sinfulness? That is probably the hardest pain to bear. It's always harder to forgive ourselves than to forgive someone else. Often the worst kind of punishment is knowing that we've hurt someone we love. Can even that be used and redeemed?

When I was a senior in high school, I started dating a young man who was several years older than I. My parents strongly disapproved and finally forbade me to see him. Thinking my world would collapse without my new love, I agreed to a plan he suggested. One spring evening, he arranged for a classmate of mine to ask me out and pick me up for a date. The classmate then took me to where my older boyfriend was waiting for me. My parents believed the lie, but I had a terrible evening, knowing that I'd deceived them. After my classmate had brought me home and had left, my father confronted me with the fact that he'd seen the classmate at the drugstore soda fountain with another girl.

"Where have you been?" he demanded.

I was trapped and I knew it, so I confessed the whole thing. Dad was furious. Mother just sat there quietly shaking her head and saying, "But I trusted you. I trusted you. I trusted you."

When I'd finished, she left the room, went into the bedroom, and closed the door. Daddy gave me a lecture, assigned some extra duties, and grounded me for two weeks. Then he went into the kitchen to get a bedtime snack.

As I walked by my parents' door on the way to my room, I could hear my gentle mother, who had always trusted me, quietly sobbing. I stood there for what seemed like an eternity, wanting to go in and put my arms around her, to tell her how sorry I was and how much I loved her, but somehow I just couldn't. Instead I went on into my room, closed the door, curled up in the fetal position on my bed, and wished that I could die.

Over the years, that memory of hurting my mother came back to me many times, but I never talked to her about it. I never told her how sorry I was. Then, after many years but sooner than I expected, the time for talking and touching and hugging was past. Mother died on January 14, 1976, with those words I had never said still bottled within me.

I don't know whether sin is a part of God's plan. That's a question for the theologians to debate. I do know that if it were not for the fact that "my sin is ever before me" (Psalm 51:3), I'm afraid that my false pride would take over. There's a selfish streak in me. I'm not as loving or as wise or as loyal as I'd like to be. I've made some really dumb mistakes in my life that keep playing over and over in my mind like broken records. For many years, this incident of hurting my mother was one of those.

Redeeming the Past

A few years ago I made an exciting discovery. Not only can God use my mistakes to draw me closer to Him, and help me to grow, but *He can take any past mistake and turn it to good.* We don't have to feel stuck in a negative condition, even if it is our own fault. God can redeem it!

One night shortly after my mother died, my Scripture reading was John 4:5–14, about Jesus' offering living water to the Samaritan woman at the well.

I closed my eyes and imagined that I was sitting on the bank of a river that was flowing with the Living Water that Jesus promised to give to all who ask. Before long, I felt moved to feed into that stream all of my worries and sinfulness and past mistakes. One by one, God called up from my memory those things that I'd been carrying for so long, and I fed each one into the river and watched it carry them all away. The first thing that came up was the time I made my mother cry. It still hurt to think of it, but I asked her forgiveness and Christ's, and then I let it go. As the river of Living Water carried it away, I sensed a great release and a forgiveness that I know was genuine.

A couple of weeks later, when we were cleaning out Mother's house, I came across her personal Bible. There were puppy tooth marks at the bottom of the scuffed leather cover. The pages, yellowed and brittled by time and use, were beginning to fall away from the binding. As I leafed through them, I found markings and dates and notations made by Mother during years and years of Bible reading. Because of my Living Water experience, I turned to John 4. That passage was starred, underlined, and dated many times. One of the dates was April 9, 1948.

Now I don't know the date of that night of my deceit, but it had to have been some time in the spring of 1948. Could April 9th have been the night I made my mother cry? And if so, could Mother's experience of the Living Water have somehow reached across all those years to heal my long-clinging brokenness? I don't know. But I believe it's possible, because in the time that is beyond time, our Lord has interwoven many patterns. And I know that His

Living Water can wash away any sorrow—even a mother's tears and a daughter's guilt after the two can no longer touch.

Since that time I've fed many sins and blunders into that stream—mistakes I've made in raising my children, times I've hurt my friends, things I've said that I wished I could take back, little lies, stupid, embarrassing things I've done—and the Living Water has borne them all away. Every now and then I repeat this prayer, and I find that besides helping me to let go of my past mistakes, it has brought about some very tangible changes for the better, both in my relationships and my circumstances. "In God's mind," wrote Madeleine L'Engle, "all acts of love are eternally present. And all that is not love can be redeemed and changed by that Love which created all."[1]

God's best for you includes the redeeming of all your past mistakes and sinfulness. If you're still carrying yours around, why not feed them into the stream of Living Water now, and let them go.

I have found one other prayer helpful in letting go of past mistakes or problems, or anything my mind tends to focus on that is troubling. The simple phrase "Only You, Lord, only You" came to me during a time when I was having a great deal of trouble with my mind wandering during prayer. Repeating that phrase whenever I noticed that my thoughts had strayed immediately restored my attention to God. It also helped me to let go of whatever the troubling thought was about. Now, whenever I find myself getting unduly attached to things, or flustered because of all I have to do, or in a state of emotional turmoil because of a disturbing situation, I try to remember to say those words in my heart: "Only You Lord, only You." Somehow they seem to break the handcuffs so that I can release whatever is troubling me.

Finding New Directions

Disappointments. Frustrations. Setbacks. Everyone has them. But I've discovered by looking in my rearview mirror that *more often than not, they've led to a change in direction that was for the better.*

There are times when the only way the Lord can get my attention to tell me I'm heading the wrong way is to slam a door in my face. Maybe that wouldn't happen so often if I listened better as I went along. It seems to me my past is filled with examples of doors slamming so that better ones could open. I've given you a few already, but I'll share another brief example here, and then I hope that you'll decide to look back at some of your own disappointments to see if they led you in new directions also.

When I was a senior in college, I became engaged to a young man from Maine. He was a likeable fellow, but we really didn't have much in common, except for the fact that we thought we couldn't live without each other. Then my fiancé flunked physics, which caused him to lose his ROTC scholarship, and that meant he'd have to return to Maine. I cried for days, begging God to let him stay in Nebraska. When it didn't happen, I raged against God. How could He be so mean as to take the love of my life away from me?

Yet after the wounds began to heal a little, the romance started to fade. With the perspective that distance provided, I could see that this young man and I were really not at all suited to each other. By the next fall, when I came to Kearney to teach, my feelings for him had cooled to the point that when a tall young architect named Rex Helleberg called me for a date, I was ready to accept.

Once you've become aware that disappointments and failures and setbacks can be guidance in disguise, maybe you'll begin to sense God's best in them, even before you can see it.

Getting the Elephant Out

Grandmother Banta once told me a story about a sculptor who was famous for his beautiful elephant statues. When a king asked him the secret of his artistry, the sculptor said, "It all starts with a huge and shapeless rock. As I study the gigantic piece of granite, slowly, very slowly, I begin to notice an outline. Gradually that outline grows stronger until finally I can see it! An elephant is stirring in there!

Then I take my chisel and my mallet and, with great singleness of purpose, I chip away every bit of stone that is not elephant."

I think what Grandmother wanted me to see was that within me there is something beautiful, a work of art, created by God. It's only been in recent years, however, that I've understood the other part of the story—that in order for the beauty to be fully expressed, all that is not beauty must be chipped away.

How marvelous to know that this "I" that often feels inadequate, afraid, angry, or just plain ugly contains within itself a thing of rarest beauty! Could it be that many of the painful things in my life are actually chisel and mallet, meant to chip away all that is not part of that God-created form?

What needs to be chipped away? Anything that gets in the way of my relationship with God. Jesus said it best: "Do not store up for yourselves treasures on earth, where moth and rust destroy, and where thieves break in and steal. But store up for yourselves treasures in heaven, where moth and rust do not destroy, and where thieves do not break in and steal. For where your treasure is, there your heart will be also" (Matthew 6:19–20 NIV).

If my bad habits or my negative thinking or my need to impress others turn me away from God, some painful chipping away may be necessary. Even things that are good—such as my career or my friendships or my volunteer work—can sometimes usurp God's place in my life. Affliction, then, can help me both to discover what my real treasures are and to let go of the rest.

I am helped in my chipping away of negative things in my life by Jesus' command and promise in Matthew 6:33. If I will seek "first the kingdom of God, and his righteousness," He says that "all these things shall be added unto [me]." If I could truly live by that verse, I wouldn't need any other rule of life. All that is necessary in this life is to seek God. He will take care of everything else. That's much easier to accept intellectually than it is to believe with the heart and to act on. But it is true.

No Impossible Situation

I don't have all the answers for the problem of suffering. But I have tried to share with you what I have learned by looking back and reflecting on my own sufferings. Perhaps the greatest thing I have learned is that although being alive inevitably involves pain and heartbreak, *there is no such thing as an impossible situation for one who draws wisdom, strength, and courage from God, and that faith is not dependent upon external events.*

Let me tell you about a young man who discovered this truth during his own suffering.

A few years ago I prayed regularly with thirteen-year-old Steven, who was dying of leukemia. One September evening, as he and I were talking on the phone, these words came to me: "Jesus said that the kingdom of God is within you, Steven. If you could peel away all the layers of skin and flesh and bones and organs that make up your body, there would still be a self that you would recognize as your own unique spirit. That part of you is untouched by sickness, or pain, or fear. It is perfect." Together Steven and I prayed that God would help him get in touch with the part of him that was perfectly well— his spirit, created in God's image. As we prayed, I heard Steven sigh, as a baby sighs when it stops crying and nestles into its mother's arms.

We finished praying and Steven said, "I have a temperature of 103, I've been vomiting all day, I'm almost blind, and I'm in terrible pain. But none of that matters!" His voice rose triumphantly. "My *spirit* doesn't have leukemia!"

Steven and I never talked again. He died a few days later, telling his parents, "Don't be afraid. I'm going to be all right."[2]

I don't know why Steven died. My vision is like that of an ant crawling around on the statue of the elephant. From my limited perspective I can't see the meaning or the form. But they are there nonetheless. Our Lord didn't cure Steven's body. Yet He gave him a genuine healing, in the priceless gift of a spirit set free to soar. Steven's short life was truly a work of art. I don't believe that any suffering is meaningless. The greatest artistic masterpieces, whether in story or symphony or painting, are always those that bear the marks of mastered ordeal. Only when I have known brokenness can I fully know the gleaming grace of wholeness.

I'm beginning to see that true freedom is not a life without problems but a spirit that rises above affliction, that an Artist's hand is at work in my life, and that His pattern will come forth out of the rock, if I allow it. I'm learning to trust the hands of the Sculptor!

God's Best Is Healing
and Wholeness

*We cannot go through life emotionally unscathed,
but God can heal our hurts.*

When I go back to visit my old hometown, I sometimes drive by the area behind my childhood home where I grieved for the baby chick that died in my hand so many years ago. I still don't have a black-and-white answer to the question, "Was it God's will that Chicken Little died?" I do feel absolutely certain of the fact that God's will is always toward life and wholeness. But sometimes the road to life and wholeness *passes through* valleys of brokenness on its way. Death clearly is part of God's plan. But early death, innocent death? I just don't know. Perhaps, in ways that are beyond my understanding, these ap-

parent injustices are also part of the charted course
that leads toward ultimate life. Yet they are never,
never without purpose, obscured though their meaning may be to our human eyes.

And what can I say about emotional pain? Is
heartsickness part of God's plan, too? I can only answer that, in order to value wholeness, one must
know what it means to be broken. I can look back,
now, on the stab wound of that early grief, and see
that in its place there is a flower with blood-red
petals, keeping open the gate to the adult woman's
heart. I think of other heart wounds: the sudden,
tragic death of Grandmother Banta when I was
eleven; Billy, the cocker spaniel that was my pal,
getting run over by a car; the broken heart that ended
my first love; the deaths, later, of my dad, my
mother, Aunt Alta. Could it be that each of these
peeled back another petal in my heart, creating open-
ings that later made it possible for compassion to
enter and take root there?

Perhaps the reason we don't have pat answers is
this: The deepest truths are always full of paradox,
fraught with apparent contradictions. It's because,
like God Himself, they cannot be reduced to logical
reasoning. Words are inadequate to convey them.

But if I could talk to that child with the dead
baby chick in her hand, I'd tell her this: Even though
you could build up scar tissue that's tough enough to
numb out future emotional pain, don't do it! It is
always God's will that his children—whether they're
nine or ninety—keep on *feeling*. Those who numb
themselves close the door against Love, who then
stands knocking, unheard. Although God doesn't

protect our hearts from all woundedness, He is *always* waiting outside the tomb of our griefs, to bind up our bleeding sores, heal our bruises, and call us back to life. It is always God's will that our hearts be healed.

Who Is Not Wounded?

Being part of an intercessory prayer group has made me very conscious of the tragedies in people's lives. Often, I've been startled to find that people I'd thought had ideal lives are bearing burdens that are almost intolerable. There is so much terrible, crushing heartsickness in the world. Clearly, no one goes through this life emotionally unscathed. We are all, to one degree or another, walking around wounded.

Yet as I've struggled through my own heartaches, I have come to know, more than ever before, that *God is a loving Father who wills that I discover overcoming!* He did not spare His own Son, but He made it possible for that Son to tell us that, yes, in this world, we will have "tribulation: but be of good cheer; I have overcome the world" (John 16:33).

Someone once wrote that "sorrow burns up a great amount of shallowness."[1] I have found that to be true for me. Emotional pain has also helped me to be less judgmental than I used to be. I've learned that I cannot change other people. Only God can do that. What I *can* do is to allow Christ the Overcomer to heal my own heart. He wants to do that even more than I want it. Like a patient first grade teacher who has to start all over with me again and again, my caring Lord teaches me, word by whispered word, to release it all to Him. Daily, He works His healing in my heart. Patiently, He is teaching me overcoming.

A Memory Transformed

We are all conditioned to a considerable extent by the experiences of our childhoods. Those early events are recorded in our minds as if on videotape, and they play and replay even when we aren't conscious of them, profoundly affecting the way we see life today and how we act and how we cope. Most of us have many warm memories of happy childhood experiences, of feeling loved and being taken care of. But no matter how happy our childhoods, each of us also has some negative tapes within us—recordings of frightening or hurtful experiences or feelings of rejection or failure. The good news is that no matter how long ago they happened, no matter how traumatic the experiences were, Christ can heal those painful memories. I know, because He has done it for me.

When I was a very little girl, I saw someone I loved very much beat a dog to death. I had not once thought about the incident in all the years since it happened. I had buried it deep, completely blocking it out of my conscious mind. Then a few years ago,

I guess the Lord decided I was finally ready to deal with it, because it came into my mind one evening during the listening part of my prayer time.

One of the things I do during my listening time is to go to some beautiful place in my imagination and meet Jesus there. That particular evening, I had met Him in a lovely mountain meadow. So I asked Him to help me heal that awful memory. Hand-in-hand, we went back to the scene of the incident and stood outside the dog pen, watching the terrible thing happening. After it was over, Jesus touched the dog, and suddenly the animal was alive again. Only now he had bright golden wings, and he rose joyfully up into the sky and flew away. Then the man who had beat the dog came over and knelt down before the Lord. Jesus touched his head and I knew in that moment that he was completely forgiven. (The man had died many years before.) Then my friend Jesus picked the child Marilyn up in His arms and carried her back to the meadow. It was a beautiful, healing experience.

Now, I know that my logical-minded readers will be saying, "A flying dog? Come on, now! It was only your imagination."

My answer is, yes! It all happened in my imagination. Thanks be to our loving God for endowing His children with the priceless gift of imagination. It's one of His favorite ways of speaking to us! When I meet Jesus in the meadow in my imagination, He is very real to me. When I ask Him to walk with me through a painful memory, if I can let go and trust Him, *He directs the flow of the mental images.* I'm sure that our Lord delights in using this way to heal our emotional scars. I believe that it can be prayer of the highest order.

After He had led me through the dog-beating episode, I asked Him to repeat it every night for a while, until the original memory was completely transformed. Now it's as if a new video has been recorded over the old one. The memory is no longer painful. The script has been rewritten!

If you are bothered by the painful memory of a traumatic experience, you, too, can find release and healing. First, try to become quiet and relaxed. Then in your imagination go to some beautiful place. Look for Jesus to meet you there. Visualize Him as clearly as you can. Feel His presence with you. Then ask Him to go back into that painful memory with you. Feel His hand in yours or His arm around you, as you go through the memory together. He will lead you. You may be quite surprised at the way in which He resolves your pain. He will transform you from within.

Peace, Be Still

It has been marvelously consoling to me to discover that Christ is very much aware of my heartaches, and that He is with me through them all. This was made unmistakably clear to me on one of the darkest nights of my life. (I want to tell you this story just as I told it in my first book.)[2]

One Sunday in 1976, less than a week before Christmas, our oldest son Paul was getting ready for an important date. I had helped him pick out a necklace for his pretty girl friend, Rita. It was her eighteenth birthday, and Paul had been so eager to find just the right gift. He left the house at 5:30 to pick her up for the dinner date. An hour later, Rita was dead and Paul was in critical condition in the intensive care unit at the hospital. His car had gone off the road at the edge of Kearney Lake (only a few blocks from our house), overturned, and struck a tree. Rita was killed instantly. Paul had a severe concussion, serious internal injuries, and deep facial cuts. For three days, he remained in a coma, hovering between life and death. We were allowed into intensive care only five minutes of every hour. The rest of the time we sat, in a state of utter shock, in a nearby waiting room.

Some time during that first night, I found my way to the hospital chapel. As I sat in the half-dark stillness, with the cries of Rita's mother still echoing in my heart and the image of Paul's battered and motionless form still before my eyes, the full horror of what had happened suddenly closed in on me.

I've always had a fear of drowning, and when I closed my eyes there in the chapel, I saw an image of a wild and storm-tossed sea, about to swallow me up in its black turbulence. Drowning in a real ocean could not have been more agonizing. I felt as if I were being strangled and I wanted to scream out my pain, but I could hardly even breathe.

And then, from somewhere in the depths of me, I heard the words, "Peace, be still." The ocean of pain that was bearing down on me began, ever so slightly, to draw back as I grabbed hold of those words. They became a life raft for me, and I held onto them, repeating them again and again, until the waves of anguish started to subside and a deep inner stillness slowly, gradually settled over me. Peace when there was no reason to feel peaceful. A gift of grace.

The words, of course, belong to Jesus. He spoke them to calm the raging sea (Mark 4:39). Now they were bubbling up from within me, to assure me of Jesus' presence with me in my anguish.

Many times in the days and nights that followed, that sea of emotion came back, again threatening to drown me. Each time it did, I closed my eyes and listened until I began to hear, once more, those calming, reassuring, life-saving words: "Peace, be still. Peace, be still." Again and again they proved to be my life raft. They did not take me away from reality. I was always very much aware of the terrible thing that had happened. At the same time I was also very much aware of God's strong, solid, sustaining hand that *would not let me sink.* I could not have stood the anguish of that time without it. It was the beginning of my healing.

There's something about emotional pain that opens up a crevice in the rock of my soul, and if I allow it to happen, Living Water flows through. That water is the very real presence of the Holy Spirit, and it cleanses me, refreshes me, and heals me. My experience during Paul's hospitalization cut through quite a bit of rock. Now I can see that the gift of Jesus' words that night was not just for me. It was meant for Paul, too.

My son was young and strong, and after his fight for life was won, his body began to heal. But there is a kind of woundedness that is beyond bones and flesh and brain cells. Paul's emotional agony was far greater than his physical pain. Rita was dead, and Paul had been the driver of the car.

When he came home from the hospital, we moved him up to the bedroom next to ours so I could be close if he needed me. Night after night, lying awake in my bed, I'd hear the low sobbing begin, and my heart would ache for my son. I'd go in and sit by his bed and pat his cheek and bathe his face with a cool cloth, binding the little boy in him back to me. But I couldn't ease his pain.

Then one night, when the sobbing began and I reached for my robe, some words shot into my mind, seemingly out of nowhere. *Get out of God's way.*

After I got over the shock of it, I realized God was telling me that there is one kind of strength Paul could find only within the lonely center of himself. That night when I went into his room, I told him about the words I had received in the hospital chapel. I told him to pray them over and over: "Peace, be still. Peace, be still."

Then I went back to my own bed. It was the hardest thing I ever had to do, to lie there, wanting to go to my grieving child and not to go. This night, as I prayed "Peace, be still," it was for Paul and not for me. I prayed the words over and over, until finally the only thing I could hear in the room next door was the deep, heavy breathing sounds of sleep.

The next morning, Paul told me that as he was falling asleep, he felt a hand touching his shoulder.

It was so physical that it startled him into wakefulness and he sat up in bed and looked around, but
there was no one in the room.

This was not the end of Paul's problems, but it
was the turning point. He learned that night to go to
God for help. He learned about the very real, this-
world presence of Christ with him. And *I* learned to
let go and trust my son's healing to Jesus, whose
loving hand had been on him all along, preparing
him to be an overcomer.

A Fresh Slant on Overcoming

I've always thought that Jesus' words, "Be of good
cheer, I have overcome the world" (John 16:33),
pertained to *His* overcoming, that the statement was
a signpost, pointing the way for each of us to overcome the world by becoming more and more like
Him. It *is* both of those things, but it's something
more, too.

One night I was praying with the Scripture in 1
John 5:4 (NIV): "For everyone born of God over-
comes the world. This is the victory that has overcome the world, even our faith." I went back from
that passage to Jesus' words: "I have overcome the
world." Could it be that He has conquered *my*
tribulations as well as His own? If so, I have to consider the fact that His words are in the *past tense.*
He's already done it! In one sense, this is not a new

thought. Other Scripture passages talk about our being "sanctified through the offering of the body of Jesus Christ *once for all*" (Hebrews 10:10, italics mine). We know that's true of our sins. But could it be that it's also true of our heartaches, those jagged rocks we stumble over in the valleys, that throw us to the ground emotionally?

As I mulled over this question, an answer came to me that I think is one of the most valuable spiritual revelations I've ever had. *Everything that happens, happens first in the spiritual realm.* Only after it has happened there does it begin to be manifest on the level of flesh and blood, earth and sky, heart and soul. That means that this earthly problem I'm facing right now (because I've given it to Him) has *already been overcome* by Jesus, in the realm of the spirit! All that is required for the overcoming to be manifest in this world of the senses is my faith. (See 1 John 5:4 again.) If I can accept that, my prayers about my problem can become thanksgivings. Instead of pleading with God, I can picture the desired outcome as having already happened in the world of the spirit and give thanks.

Whatever your problem is today, remind yourself that everything happens first in the realm of the spirit. Try to realize that because you've given your problem to Christ, it has already been overcome in the Spirit. And give thanks from the deep, deep part of your heart. I believe that it is from just such prayer plug-ins that worldly conditions may begin to reflect their already existing spiritual perfections. *Thy will be done, O Lord, on earth as it already is in heaven.*

Placing the Blame

I recently heard a physician say that at the base of every physical problem, if you look for it long enough and diligently enough, you'll find that there is a problem of unforgiveness.

Well, I don't know. That's a pretty sweeping statement, and I'm not sure that I can accept it without exception. But the doctor went on to say something that I do definitely believe is true. He said, "The person who holds a grudge is poisoning himself as surely as if he drank a cupful of arsenic." *This* I believe is true, and it's a poison that affects not only the physical body but also the soul and the spirit.

So what can we do? Every one of us has been wronged in some way. Maybe our parents abused us, or our spouse was unfaithful to us, or a co-worker started an untrue rumor about us. How can we help resenting, blaming, holding a grudge? Isn't that just a natural human response to being mistreated? Yes. It is natural. But until I stop blaming, I cannot truly approach God. In His Sermon on the Mount, Jesus said, "So if you are standing before the altar in the Temple, offering a sacrifice to God, and suddenly remember that a friend has something against you, leave your sacrifice there beside the altar and go and apologize and be reconciled to him, and then come and offer your sacrifice to God" (Matthew 5:23, 24 TLB). Jesus doesn't mention anything about what the other person ought to do. He says to me, "*You* go." He doesn't enter into a debate about who is at fault. That doesn't matter one bit! He is concerned with *my* health of body, soul, and spirit! But how in the world can I get rid of my hurt feelings, my resentments, my grudges?

Let me first admit that although I am not perfectly free from these negative emotions, I'm working on it, with the Lord's help. There is one thing that has aided me more than anything else in this work on myself. It is Laura Huxley's statement that "You are not the target."[3]

I'll have to go back to my childhood again, to explain why this has helped me so much. Most of the time, my mother was a very loving and nurturing parent. But whenever she got mad at me for any reason, her way of punishing me was simply not to speak to me for a while. Sometimes this went on for days on end, as I followed her around, crying, begging, pleading for her to recognize my existence and to forgive me. She would continue to act as if I weren't even there. Unless you have experienced this in childhood, you may not be able to realize how devastating it is to a youngster. I'm sure, now, that Mother didn't realize what it was doing to me. Anyway, when I began taking psychology courses in college, I discovered that this form of emotional abandonment can cause serious psychological problems in a person's life. I'd already held a great amount of resentment toward Mother for many years because of those episodes of the silent treatment, and what I learned in my psychology courses just seemed to make it worse.

Years later, in counseling, I discovered that my experience with my mother was the major contributor to the fact that I'd always had difficulty being assertive enough with my own children. To have someone that I loved be angry with me was so painful that I just couldn't bear it. It all stemmed from that old fear of being emotionally abandoned. Of course, this further increased my grudge toward my mother. She was a wonderful person in many, many ways, and most of the time she was extremely loving and caring. But there was that one thing, and it was getting in the way of my relationships with my children and with my God. I had to deal with it.

About that time I came across a book by Ira Progoff, entitled *At a Journal Workshop.*[4] One of the exercises Progoff suggests is that you have a dialogue in your journal with someone with whom you've had some relationship problems. It doesn't matter whether the individual is living or dead (my mother had been dead several years at the time). After I got into a relaxed state of mind, I asked the Holy Spirit to direct the dialogue, and then began to write. I told Mother in my journal that I love her—because I do, very much. Then I wrote out a number of questions about why she had treated me the way she had when I was a child. The answers that came spilling out onto the page were real wake-ups for me. As I read them over, I sensed a validity in them. They *fit* with what I knew about my mother and the family she grew up in. The answers came not from the spirit world, but from my own intuitive knowledge—long buried—of who Mother was and of her life and relationships.

They were there in my inner mind, but I'd never let them into my conscious mind before.

For instance, the dialogue brought out the fact that Mother had always felt somewhat inferior to one of her sisters. She had found that not speaking to her sister gave her some power over her, temporarily bringing back a little of Mother's ailing self-esteem. When she had treated *me* that way, it was an attempt (probably unconscious) to assure herself that she was not losing *my* love! My crying and begging for her attention provided her with reassurance that I really did love her. Anyway, what this whole experience brought out for me was that Mother did what she did because *she* had some feelings of being unloved! It placed the whole relationship between Mother and me in a new light. I was able to truly and sincerely forgive her.

Since then, in other instances in which people have treated me badly, I'm beginning to be able to see that in one way or another, *the people who have wounded me are wounded people themselves.* That is a healing thought. I can remind myself that *I am not the real target!*

Prayerful, written dialogue with those who have hurt you is a great help in overcoming emotional pain. Another is to imagine yourself in a situation in which someone you are unable to forgive needs your help—perhaps your sister-in-law. What would you do if she had just been struck by a car and you saw her lying on the street in front of you, wounded and bleeding? Of course you'd call for help, and then you'd probably kneel down by her and try to comfort her. Your heart would truly go out to her.

Well, maybe she really is bleeding—deep inside.

Maybe the bleeding has been going on all her life, so she's learned to reject other people before they can reject her. Maybe that's why she has rejected or hurt you. Maybe she is starved for love but afraid to show it. If you knew that to be true, could you stop blaming her for what she has done to you? Could you be a big enough person to have compassion and do what you can to stop her internal bleeding? Could you pray for her emotional healing? Doing so is your best hope for restoring your own.

Maybe just saying those words, "I am not the target," when your brother-in-law or a neighbor says something that hurts your feelings will help you. It's a recognition that there are unconscious forces at work in that person that cause him to try to hurt you, something or someone in his past that he's trying to get even with—not you. Visualizing him wounded and bleeding will help make you aware of the pain out of which he acted when he hurt you.

Whatever you can do that will help you stop blaming, do it for the health of your body, your soul, and, especially, your spirit.

But What if You're the Guilty One?

Although it's vital that we work on forgiving others who have in some way mistreated us, there's someone else who may be standing in the wings, still very much in need of forgiveness. That person is you or

I. Perhaps you've had the experience of apologizing and asking someone for forgiveness, making all possible amends, and yet the person you wronged still refuses to forgive you. What then? Then it is that person's problem. It is no longer yours or mine. We have to let go, always keeping the door open for a future reconciliation, but not torturing ourselves with guilt in the meantime. I've had to accept the fact that, at least in one particular instance, the reconciliation may never happen. So I *have* to let go. My friend, Jesus, is the only One who can truly free me from this kind of situation.

After we've apologized and done everything we can to right a wrong we've committed, *it is God's will that we accept His forgiveness and that we forgive ourselves.*

Most of us, I suspect, are carrying around some old guilts. If that is true of you, listen to some of the most comforting words in the Bible. They are from 1 John 3:19, 20 NIV. "This then is how . . . we set our hearts at rest in his presence whenever our hearts condemn us. For God is greater than our hearts, and he knows everything." When does my heart condemn me? When I become painfully aware of my weaknesses, as well as my sinfulness. My heart condemns me for being a fool, a weakling, sometimes vain, often prideful. My heart condemns me when I'm not loving enough to my husband, or when I say some dumb thing. (And how often I do that last one!) But God, who is so much greater than my condemning heart, knows all the awful things about me that I'd rather hide. He knows what I'm thinking at every moment. But He's saying, "I am not easily shocked or disgusted. I know you better than you know yourself, including all your shortcomings and sinfulness, and I love you anyway. You have asked me to forgive all your sins, and you're trying to be a better person. So quit your groveling. Quit whipping yourself. You are my beloved child. Put your hand in mine and accept my forgiveness and let me help you to get on with your life."

To be able to tell someone else about my sinfulness and to pray together about it is a tremendous help for me. It is a way to inner healing recommended in the Bible. "Admit your faults to one another . . . so you may be healed" (James 5:16 TLB). But it is not easy to allow ourselves to be vulnerable to another. I think we're all at least a little afraid that the other person, once aware of our secret sins, will stop loving us. Of course, it's important to choose someone we trust, a person who is discreet and who will not discuss with others what we've said in private. Yet once we've broken through our resistance, we're very likely to find that our friend loves us even more because of our honest sharing.

If you've had trouble fully accepting God's forgiveness, your minister may be the best one to take your guilts to. He or she can pray with you in a way that will help you to know, deep inside, that the Lord has truly forgiven you.

Another thing that has helped me to let go of my guilt feelings is to write in my journal about them. I begin with a prayer, asking the Holy Spirit to help me to examine my conscience. Then I list the wrongs I feel I've committed.

The first time I did this, I included a number of excuses and alibis, and I omitted some of the things that were most painful. But as I've continued to do it (about once a week), I've gradually learned to be more honest with God. Why try to hide anything? He already knows it, anyway! This is definitely *not* dwelling on the negative. It is getting the garbage out so that Christ can deal with it, and the results are amazingly positive.

I conclude my journal entry by writing out a prayer, asking for God's forgiveness for these and any hidden sins, known only to Him. The prayer always ends with thanksgiving that I am, indeed, completely forgiven, and that I am free, free, *free.* You may want to destroy the paper on which you've written the exercise. That way, as you write, you'll feel freer, knowing that you and your friend, Jesus, will be the only ones to read it.

The Weakness That Remains

What about that weakness I have that just won't go away, no matter how hard I pray or how many people I forgive or how diligently I have worked with Jesus to heal my memories? When I come up against one of these, I remember that Jesus gives us the only answer in His words, "My grace is sufficient for thee: for my strength is made perfect in weakness" (2 Corinthians 12:9).

At a retreat not long ago I talked to a woman who had been physically abused by her father when she was a child. No matter what she did, she couldn't seem to forgive him. But as a devout Christian, she knew that her inability to forgive was standing between her and God. Finally, one night in desperation, she prayed, "Lord, You know that I *don't want* to forgive him! What's more, I *can't* do it! All I can pray for at this point is that *You will make me willing.*" Even though it didn't happen instantly, she told me, things began to take place in her life that gradually helped her to let go of her old resentment. She found that Christ's strength worked through her weakness, to heal her heart.

Sometimes I am tempted to think, in regard to my weaknesses, "Not even Almighty God can handle this!" Yet there is nothing that God cannot handle—or will not handle, if it needs to be done. Maybe my weakness is there to keep reminding me that I *must* rely on Him. My flawed nature helps me to become *consciously dependent* upon my heavenly Father. It simplifies my belief, making me more childlike in my relationship with Him. When I realize this, there is but one thing for me to do—fall on my knees in thanksgiving.

My all-powerful heavenly Father, I know that it is Your will that my heart be healed, and that Your Presence has never, never left me, no matter how weak or lost I may have felt. I thank You for Your Son, who is in my every pain with me, and for the Holy Spirit, who breathes His healing breath over my woundedness, making me whole and setting me free. Amen.

11

God's Best Is Being One in Christ

*Reap spiritual rewards from involvement
with others.*

Finding God's best is a lifelong quest. We have begun it, you and I, when we have come to know in a solid way that there is a reliable power directing our lives, and when we have discovered that God's will is:

not a mysterious process but an everyday attitude,
not burdensome but glorious,
not a restrictor but an enabler,
not a weight to be endured but a promise to be
embraced.

Once we know that these truths are valid in our own individual lives, another realization begins to rise in our hearts like the early morning sun. It is this: *God's best for you and for me most certainly rests on His best for all of His creation.* We begin to sense that there is a unity so deep and so profound that it goes beyond yesterday, beyond today, even beyond tomorrow. We begin to develop a new sense of ourselves as joined with others and with God.

After James and John had seen Jesus transfigured on Mount Tabor, our Lord led them right back down from the mountain into the world again to deal with pain and suffering (Matthew 17:1–9). After you and I have begun to experience God's best for us personally, He always leads us out into the world, to be together in new and transforming ways. Like Paul after Christ appeared to him on the road to Damascus, we have been given *new sight.*

> Placing his hands on Saul [Ananias] said, "Brother Saul, the Lord—Jesus, who appeared to you on the road as you were coming here—has sent me so that you may see again, and be filled with the Holy Spirit." Immediately something like scales fell from Saul's eyes and he could see again. He got up and was baptized (Acts 9:17, 18 NIV).

New Eyes

Some people I know are seeing with new eyes even now, are beginning to sense that "my Father's house" is an eternal reality that can be glimpsed, even in this life.

After church services at Mt. Carmel Nursing Home on Thursday mornings, I wheel a bright little lady who is in her nineties back to her room. All the way down the hall, she tells me what a wonderful place this is. Each time we meet another resident, she says, "This is my dear friend Gladys . . . Esther . . . Philip." She invites me into her room and shows me pictures of her children and grandchildren, introduces me to the nurses and the women who clean. Recently she told me that she loves her room so much she's made the head sister promise that when she's gone, she'll give it to someone who will love it as much as she does.

The last time I wheeled her back, I asked her how it was that she was able to see good in everyone and everything. Mrs. Elliot thought a minute and then replied, "Well, I'm a very old lady and I'll soon be crossing over. I guess the Lord just saw fit to give me my heavenly eyes a wee bit early."

I think her comment delighted her as much as it did me, because I could hear her chuckling to herself as I walked all the way back down the hall.

Yes, it's *the way we see* that makes all the difference. The awareness of our oneness in Christ will come when you and I begin to practice looking through our heavenly eyes. Just as the cells of my brain and those of my big toe are separate yet part of one body, so you and I are part of a single spiritual body. Just as we share the air we breathe, the earth that supports us, and the silent beauty of the starlit sky, we also share an invisible bond of spirit.

Tipping the Balance

Ultimately, I believe, it will be the tiny, personal acts of love and caring that will swing the balance, create the chain reaction, wake us up to our oneness in Christ. People reaching out to people, touching, caring, bringing hope. Such acts happen every day, but most of the time we don't know them for what they really are—one part of this body we share, serving another part, as a hand feeding a mouth. That is, until something happens to jar us awake, as it did to me one night on my way from Nebraska to our summer cabin in Colorado.

I'd been driving in pouring rain all day, sometimes barely able to see the road ahead. It was a long, slow trip. (Instead of the usual eight hours, it took me almost twelve.) Twenty-four miles out of Colorado Springs, I had a blowout. The next thing I knew, I was in a ditch, with a ruined front tire, no jack handle, and an inflatable spare I didn't know how to use.

Fortunately the car was still drivable. I pulled out of the ditch, turned on my hazard lights, and waited—fifteen minutes, a half hour, an hour. Cars sped past on the Interstate from both directions, not even slowing down. I didn't really blame them. It's dangerous to stop when you don't know what you might be getting into. Anyway, it was forty degrees and pouring rain. Who'd want to change someone else's tire in that ice cold shower bath?

Finally, after an hour and a half, a dilapidated

old car stopped, and a young man with long hair, ragged jeans, and no coat got out. In no time at all, he had the tire changed, inflated, and ready to go. When he finished he was soaked to the skin. I tried to hand him some cash, but he absolutely refused to accept it, no matter how hard I insisted.

That was when he said the words that jarred me awake: "Please. I want to do this as an act of thanksgiving. I just got out of prison in Michigan and I'm so glad to be on my way home. Just do something nice for someone else when you get the chance." And he got into his car and drove away.

I couldn't help wondering what he'd been in for and where his home was. But of one thing I felt sure: No matter whether he drove north or south, east or west, that young man's life was now heading in the right direction. Giving of self. Involvement. Christ's way. On that cold, rainy night on the road to Colorado, I suddenly knew that I had met the good Samaritan, and that he was asking me to be the same to someone else in need.

During the rest of my drive, I alternately prayed for that young man and thanked God for him. For at least one brief chunk of time we had not been ex-con and stranded woman, but one part of an invisibly shared body helping another part.

The young man's idea of passing on kindness could really make a difference in our world. If each of us would make it a practice to do something nice for someone else whenever we've received a favor, who knows how far the chain might reach.

The next day, as I sat on the cabin porch thinking about the young man who had changed my tire, I heard, in the distance, the bells of the old village church. It wasn't Sunday, and they don't ring on the hour. Maybe it was a wedding. At any rate, their sound, a reminder of ritual, stirred a question in me—one I've looked at from changing perspectives at various times in my life.

Do I Really Need Church?

The Bible clearly directs us, as followers of Jesus Christ, to gather together. "Let us hold fast the profession of our faith without wavering; (for he is faithful that promised). And let us consider one another to provoke unto love and to good works: *Not forsaking the assembling of ourselves together*" (Hebrews 10:23–25, italics mine).

There have been times in my life when I *have* forsaken the assembling together, times when I have seriously questioned the value of church membership and participation. At one point, I decided that all ritual was just show, detracting from the real message of the gospel. Since I was raised in a rather formal church, I began to shop around and spent some time migrating from one denomination to another. For a while, I even convinced myself that I could lead a truly Christ-centered life without going to *any* church. But gradually, I began to feel an emptiness—a deep spiritual loneliness that simply wouldn't go away. It was a homesickness for "my Father's house."

When I finally found my way back to the church

of my childhood, I discovered something marvelous. The faith that had been handed to me by others and later cast aside finally *belonged* to me. It was mine by choice now and, like the prodigal son, I was *glad* to be home again! The rituals no longer seemed empty. I appreciated them, but in a fresh way.

The rituals of every church have great value because they lift us out of our daily ruts and wake us up to a meaningfulness that we're apt to forget during the rest of the week. Human beings have always surrounded their important occasions with as much beauty and loveliness, ceremony and ritual as possible. In this way, the special days can help to transform the ordinary ones. A birthday party is a way of celebrating the gift of each other; so is a wedding anniversary celebration. On Sundays, we celebrate the gift of Christ to us. Ritual says to me: There is meaning here; there is great significance; grace and illumination are real. It's true that the meaning and the significance and the grace are real, whether they are surrounded by ritual or not. But I would never say to my daughter on her birthday, "Well, we know you were born. And (imagine that!) you're still here. Now it's time for us both to get back to our daily work."

After a week of work and before another of the same, I want some moments of high inspiration in a place that radiates a quiet beauty. I want my moments in God's house to be a little finer, a little more uplifting, a little more solemn than my everyday moments. I want that home-again feeling I get when I recognize a certain amount of tradition that has been preserved for me from the faith of my fathers. I want to know that I am part of a shared Body, because that awareness drives away the spiritual loneliness I sometimes feel. Worshiping in my church provides these things for me . . . and so much more.

Recently we had two weddings and a graduation in our extended family. I noticed an interesting thing when we all got together. It seems to happen every time. We always talk through the same shared experiences of the past—the happy ones, the funny ones, and the sad ones, even though we've discussed them all before and everyone knows what's coming next.

I'll bet your family does that, too. Why do we do it? Wouldn't it be much easier to let the painful memories fall into oblivion? No. Each time those dreadful moments are talked through from the safe perspective of *a people who have passed through them,* they lose a little of their horror. These, along with the moments of great joy and shared funny incidents, become a focal point around which family warmth collects because they represent a drawing together, a time when we were *us.* When those significant events happened, they lifted us out of the daily routine that causes us to live unconsciously most of the time. Those significant moments *woke us up* and made us realize that life matters. Reliving them brings back a little of that wakefulness.

There is a parallel between this family thing we do and the Jews' telling and retelling their history as a people, until it was finally written down and became the Old Testament. And of our reliving, in the sequence of the Christian liturgical year, the birth, life, death, and resurrection of Christ.

I guess it all has to do, once again, with that invisible linking, that fusing of the many into the One Body of Christ. Oh yes. I do need my church.

"That They All May Be One"

On the night of our Lord's arrest, He prayed to His Father, "That they all may be one; as thou, Father, art in me, and I in thee, that they also may be one in us" (John 17:21).

Well, that's a nice hope. Yet I am painfully aware that our world has known more violence and terrorism during the past few years than ever before, and that there are precious few signs that world crises will be resolved without a great amount of further pain and anguish.

Still I do not think it is naïve to hope, to believe, that perhaps these horrible things could be birthing pains for a new order of Oneness in Christ that is about to break forth. Perhaps that time is closer than we think. Maybe it awaits only our recognition of its reality! Could it be, in fact, that just such oneness was *built into creation by our Maker* . . . and that He's been waiting these long eons for us to wake up to it?

> Having made known unto us the mystery of his will
> . . . that in the dispensation of the fulness of times he
> might gather together in one *all things* in Christ, both
> which are in heaven, and which are on earth
> (Ephesians 1:9, 10, italics mine).

Before that gathering together can become visible in our world, we need to know and affirm that we are united in our hearts, even though our forms of worship differ. We need to reach across the spaces that separate us, and allow ourselves to become one in spirit.

There was a time when I thought that all Christian denominations should get together and become one church, but I've changed my mind about that. There are many different kinds of people in the world, so there will probably always be a need for different ways of worshiping the same Lord. To me, the idea of condemning others because they don't belong to my denomination is about as un-Christian as one can get. As Madeleine L'Engle puts it, "It is a presumptuous thing, and a very seductive one, to decide that you and your group are the sheep destined for heaven, and that all the rest . . . are destined for hell fire."[1]

We can preserve our different ways of worshiping, and still be Christ's one body! Although I'm not a Roman Catholic, I have often attended a prayer group that meets in the Catholic chapel at our local college. Men and women from all denominations come together there, to sing to God, to praise Him, and to pray as one. A warm spiritual closeness has developed in that group, even though Sunday morning finds the members worshiping in many different churches. *We can hold hands across the spaces between us!*

A few years ago, in a rural Kansas area, a tiny girl wandered off into the wheat fields and got lost. The frantic parents called all their neighbors, who began searching the acres of wheat. Temperatures were blistering and, of course, the child had no water, so they searched, even all through the night, but without success.

The next day, someone suggested that to be sure of covering every foot of the tall wheat acreage, the searchers should *hold hands* and walk together, sweeping through the fields one portion at a time. In this way, they did find the little girl, but I'm sorry to have to tell you that they were too late. She had died of heat stroke. I can still see the agonized face of that poor mother, whose picture appeared in our paper. Her words, quoted in the caption, still haunt me: "If only we had held hands sooner."

O Lord Christ, teach us, Your children, to reach through our stained glass barricades and hold hands, while there is still time. Teach us to emphasize the principles that unify us and be accepting of the spaces between us. Help us to reach past labels such as Protestant and Catholic . . . even past labels such as Jew, Hindu, and Moslem. Let us join hands for the sake of this precious but delicate planet You have created for us. Teach us that there isn't any "they." That there is only "we." Take my hand, Lord. Stretch my arm. In Your holy name I pray. Amen.

It Is Already Happening

Being one in Christ means seeing with our heavenly eyes. Our world has been sick for a long time, but I believe that more and more people are becoming awakened to the unity we share in spirit. Even though there is still great darkness in the world, I believe that the overall vision of mankind is just on the edge of making a dramatic shift toward wholeness. As a mother here, an uncle there, a teacher or pastor or president someplace else wakes up to God's plan to bring *all things* together in Christ, that vision will be *caught* by their children, their friends, their spouses, their pupils, even their governments! It is happening already.

All over the world, people are beginning to sense that they are part of Something bigger. They are becoming more nearly attuned to a very real dimension of order and harmony in the universe. Sometimes it's just one or two kindred spirits who meet to pray with their Bibles, or it might be a larger group gathering for prayer and praise, or even a few friends sitting together in the silence, listening for the still small voice of God. Into these little pockets of fellowship in Christ there enters a new awareness of the Holy Spirit. And slowly, irreversibly, their lives are transformed, and individuals begin to discover a sense of collective purpose, unblocked by artificial divisions.

It is perhaps in souls such as these that the seed crystals of lasting world peace will be planted. If we believe Jesus, you and I should be among these, because the first recorded saying of our Lord in the Gospel of Mark is, "The time is fulfilled, and the kingdom of God is at hand" (Mark 1:15). It has taken us nearly two thousand years to *begin* to recognize that as an already accomplished fact. On the level of the spirit, the kingdom of God has already come to the earth and awaits only our recognition of it!

If you and I believe that "the kingdom of God is at hand," we can be channels through which the spiritual reality may enter into physical form, in the everywhere-present Spirit of God. If we can attune ourselves with His will, through daily prayer and obedience, we will dwell together in the bond of the One Spirit of God, and that unity will overflow into the world around us. Already, we who dwell together in that One Spirit are touching one another in more ways than we can ever guess. Whether we realize it or not, *what goes on at the center of our individual lives will have a profound effect upon the international situation.* Even your smallest act of loving concern sends out ripples that may touch the lives of people you've never met! Glory and freedom will come through caring.

How to Pray for Our World

During a question-and-answer period at a recent prayer retreat I co-led, a young man asked, "How can I pray for the good of the world? I don't understand politics or SALT treaties or the current oil glut. I really don't *know* what to pray for. I can pray for peace, but that seems so vague."

The only answer I could give was one arising from my own similar lack of understanding about the intricacies of world affairs. The best way I can pray for our scarred world is to see it as God created it, to visualize fields of green wheat swaying in the wind, life-giving rivers flowing seaward, clean, clear smog-less skies, and men and women everywhere beating "their swords into plowshares, and their spears into pruning hooks." With Isaiah, I can affirm every day that "nation shall not lift up sword against nation, neither shall they learn war any more" (Isaiah 2:4).

Perhaps I can best pray for our world by planting something, such as the blue spruce my grandfather planted that still points my eyes toward heaven, or by teaching a child how to listen for God's voice, or by feeding a hummingbird, knowing that in doing these things, I am affirming the validity of God's creation. I am saying Yes! to God, echoing the Yes! of His Son, Jesus Christ.

> The Son of God, the Christ Jesus that we proclaimed among you . . . was never Yes and No: with him it was always Yes, and however many the promises God made, the Yes to them all is in him (2 Corinthians 1:20 JB).

I believe that as more and more people begin to hold hands in Spirit, our collective heavenly eyes will begin to look *through* the appearance of both human good and human evil, to behold the spiritual reality that has always been there. And we *will* be part of God's voice as He sings His undefeatable Yes!

God's Best

I hope that my reflections on my experiences have encouraged you to look for God's patterns in your own life. It is easy to get too caught up in the events of the moment to think about patterns, but they are there nonetheless. God does have blueprints for His creation and for every individual within it. Although baby chickens sometimes die and people often hurt the ones they love the most, although terrible tragedies occur, and pain and suffering are rampant, life does most certainly have meaning and purpose. I am convinced that no flaw of mine and no despair of mine could possibly alter the glory of the Creator's plan. God is in control of His universe today, tomorrow and always.

Our Lord said, "I am . . . the bright and morning star" (Revelation 22:16).

Like the wise men who followed the star in the east, we who seek God's best will find it when we truly follow Jesus. His best will reveal itself in fresh ways as we open ourselves to it in daily prayer, listening for His guidance and living His leadings. Our choices will become clearer, our lives more creative and authentic, and our work more meaningful. We'll be able to pass through our pain and suffering, into a new kind of wholeness . . . a wholeness wrought by hands that clasp across spaces broader than a Kansas wheat field, and by little acts of caring rippling out until they touch the first bright rays of the Morning Star.

APPENDIX

Scriptural References for Closing Statements of Chapter One

Even though there are many things I do not understand about God's will, there *are* certain things that I *know* are part of His plan for my life. Some of them are obvious. He wants me to . . .

- love Him enough to put Him first in my life (Matthew 6:33);
- keep human love in my life, too (John 13:34);
- abide by His moral laws (Exodus 20:1–17);
- tell others about Him (Matthew 19:20) gently, never trying to force my beliefs on them, remembering that example is the best teacher (1 Timothy 4:12);

- be a servant, first to Him (Psalm 100:2) and then to others whom He gives me to serve (Mark 9:35);
- recognize my dependence upon Him (Proverbs 3:5,6);
- have a deep reverence for the Bible (John 5:39);
- honor His sacrifice by coming to His communion table (Luke 22:19).

Some things He wills are not so obvious. He wills . . .

- that there be challenges and growth (and therefore some pain and suffering) in my life (John 16:33);
- that my scars and wounds be healed; that I discover overcoming (1 Peter 2:24);
- that I offer Jesus my pain and failures, uniting them to His suffering (1 Peter 5:10);
- that I not shut off my feelings (Psalm 25:17–18);
- that I spend time with Him every day (Proverbs 8:34), not so that I may get the things I want, but so that I may come to know Him better and love Him more (Matthew 6:33);
- that I *live creatively* (Mark 4:26–29), aware of His presence within me (Colossians 1:27);
- that I be free, in the sense of Galatians 5:1 ("Stand fast therefore in the liberty wherewith Christ hath made us free.");
- that I be true to myself—the self He gave me (1 Thessalonians 2:3–4);
- that I have work to do that I find satisfying (Mark 13:34);

- that I ask for His help with my decisions (James 1:5)
- that I keep searching for answers to the unanswerable, for as long as I live (2 Timothy 2:15);
- that I make room in my thinking for apparent inconsistencies, knowing that they may lead me to higher truths (1 Corinthians 13:12);
- that I can pray, "Thy will to be done," without a sense of resignation to the worst (Psalm 37:3).

In return for my seeking His best, God offers me some gifts:

... increased confidence that life is ultimately meaningful, that He really is in control (Ephesians 1:9–11);

... new perspectives on pain and suffering, resulting in a growing ability to cope (Romans 8:18, 28, 31);

... new tools for making decisions and receiving His guidance (James 1:5, Psalm 32:8);

... a remedy for the disease of emptiness (Deuteronomy 33:27);

... the discovery that the Holy Spirit is a flowing Stream within me (John 7:37–39), who understands who I am and what I need and knows how to move me toward realization of my God-given potential (John 16:13);

... an eagle-winged awareness that *all* experiences have meaning (Ecclesiastes 3:1–8);

... awareness that there is no such thing as an impossible situation for one who draws wisdom, strength, and courage from God (Matthew-19:26).

. . . the solid conviction that God's will is not burdensome but glorious, not a restrictor but an
enabler, not a stagnant pond but a flowing River
(Proverbs 8).

Notes

1 *What is God's Best?*

1. Benedict J. Groeschel, *Spiritual Passages* (New York: Crossroad Publishing Company, 1986), p. 192.

2 *God's Best in Your Choices*

1. Richard Schneider, " 'I Will Not Let You Fail,' " *Guideposts,* August 1981, pp. 2–7.
2. Madeleine L'Engle, *A Circle of Quiet* (New York: Seabury Press, 1972), p. 201.

3 *God's Best Means Being True to Yourself*

1. Francis Martin, *Touching God* (Denville, NJ: Dimension Books, 1975), pp. 42–43.

2. Arthur Gordon, *A Touch of Wonder* (Old Tappan, NJ: Fleming H. Revell, 1974), p. 218.
3. Meister Eckhart, trans. Raymond Blakney.
4. Garry Friesen, *Decision Making and the Will of God* (Portland: Multnomah Press, 1980).
5. A version of this dream incident previously appeared in my book, *Beyond TM: A Practical Guide to The Lost Traditions of Christian Meditation* (Mahwah, NJ: Paulist Press, 1980), pp. 105–6.
6. M. M. Helleberg, *Your Hearing Loss* (Chicago: Nelson-Hall, 1979).

4 *Finding God's Best For You*

1. This section appeared in abbreviated form as "How to Be a Daily Pray-er" in *Guideposts,* May 1982, p. 28.
2. William Temple, source unknown.
3. For other books on prayer, see the section, "Suggestions for Further Reading," starting on page 250.

5 *God's Best Means Saying Yes to Life*

1. Madeleine L'Engle, *Walking on Water* (Wheaton, IL: Harold Shaw, 1980), p. 13.
2. Elizabeth O'Connor, *Eighth Day of Creation* (Waco, Texas: Word Books, 1971), p. 21.
3. Marcus Bach, *The World of Serendipity* (Marina del Rey, California: DeVorss and Company, 1970), pp. 2–3.
4. This incident appeared originally in Marilyn Morgan Helleberg, *Where Soul and Spirit Meet* (Nashville: Abingdon Press, 1986), p. 35.

6 *God's Best in Your Work*

1. Malcolm Muggeridge, *Something Beautiful for God* (New York: Harper & Row, 1971).

2. Sylvia Hellman, source unknown.
3. Abraham Lincoln's record is cited by James Keller, "Failure Isn't Fatal" in *Words to Live By* (New York: Simon and Schuster, 1959), pp. 43–44.

7 *God's Best Means Living Creatively*

1. Frances G. Wickes, *The Inner World of Choice* (New York: Harper & Row, 1963), cited by Elizabeth O'Connor in *Eighth Day of Creation*, p. 91.
2. Johann Wolfgang von Goethe, cited by Virginia W. Bass in *Dimensions of Man's Spirit* (Los Angeles: Science of Mind Publications, 1975), p. 109.
3. Elizabeth O'Connor, *Eighth Day of Creation*, p. 87.
4. Philip Goldberg, *The Intuitive Edge* (Boston: Houghton Mifflin, 1983), p. 177.

8 *God's Best for You in Loving*

1. Harold Hill with Irene Burk Harrell, *How to Live in High Victory* (Plainfield, NJ: Logos International, 1977), chapter 10.

9 *God's Best, Even in the Darkness*

1. Madeleine L'Engle, *And It Was Good* (Wheaton, Illinois: Harold Shaw Publishers, 1983), p. 169.
2. This story originally appeared in Helleberg, *Where Soul and Spirit Meet*, pp. 17–18.

10 *God's Best Is Healing and Wholeness*

1. *Forward Day by Day*, (Cincinnati, OH: Forward Movement Publications, Feb/Mar, 1986).
2. This incident is told in Marilyn Morgan Helleberg, *Beyond TM*, pp. 87–89.

3. Laura Archera Huxley, *You Are Not the Target* (North Hollywood: Wilshire, 1970).
4. Ira Progoff, *At a Journal Workshop* (New York: Dialogue House Library, 1975), pp. 210–227.

11 *God's Best Is Being One in Christ*

1. Madeleine L'Engle, *And It Was Good,* p. 154.

Suggestions for Further Reading

Books on Prayer

As I started to prepare this list of books on prayer, I realized that there was no way I could possibly include all of the books that have been valuable to me in my own study of prayer, let alone the many other fine books that I *haven't* read! So these are just a few that you may want to add to your own list of books that are meaningful to you.

Daily Devotionals

Daily Guideposts. Carmel, New York: Guideposts Books. This is a compilation of devotionals written by contemporary authors, using an anecdotal style. A new edition is published each year.

Forward Day-by-Day. Cincinnati: Forward Movement Publications. Devotionals are based on lectionary readings for each day. Authors are anonymous.

Quiet Hour, The. Elgin, Illinois: David C. Cook. Readers are asked to read a passage of Scripture, and the meditation for the day is based on a single verse from that reading.

Upper Room, The. Nashville: The Upper Room. Short readings that begin with Scripture and end with a prayer and a "Thought for the Day."

Meditational Prayer

Brooke, Avery. *Hidden in Plain Sight.* Nashville: The Upper Room, 1986. An easy-to-understand book about Christian meditation.

Helleberg, Marilyn Morgan. *A Guide to Christian Meditation.* New York: Walker and Company, 1980. A step-by-step guide to a deepening relationship with Christ through meditative prayer.

Johnston, William, editor. *The Cloud of Unknowing.* Garden City: Doubleday Image Books, 1973. This is by an anonymous fourteenth-century Christian mystic. It is for the serious student who is ready for deeper contemplation.

Kelsey, Morton. *The Other Side of Silence.* Mahwah, NJ: Paulist Press, 1976. An extensive and detailed treatment of the subject of Christian meditation.

Lawrence, Brother. *The Practice of the Presence of God.* Old
Tappan, NJ: Fleming H. Revell Company, 1958.
Contains the simple wisdom of a seventeenth-century
monk who felt the constant companionship of God.

Merton, Thomas. *Contemplative Prayer.* Garden City:
Doubleday Image Books, 1969. Using Scripture texts
and writings of Christian spiritual leaders of the past,
Merton applies time-tested methods to modern life.

Pennington, Basil M. *Daily We Touch Him.* Garden City:
Doubleday Image Books, 1979. A practical manual of
spiritual exercises.

Way of a Pilgrim, The. New York: Seabury Press, 1965.
Written anonymously in the mid-nineteenth century,
this is the account of the life of a "wanderer-in-Christ"
who practiced the Prayer of the Heart. It is for the
serious student of contemplative prayer.

Prayer—General

Green, Thomas H. *Opening to God.* Notre Dame, IN: Ave
Maria Press, 1977. Fr. Green makes the exercises of the
great spiritual writers intelligible to the average reader
who sincerely wants to grow in the ability to pray.

Hasbrouk, Hypatia. *Handbook of Positive Prayer.* Unity Village,
MO: Unity Books, 1984. A discussion and guide to
various types of affirmative prayer.

Higgins, John J. *Thomas Merton on Prayer.* Garden City:
Doubleday Image Books, 1975. A comprehensive study
of Merton's thoughts on prayer.

Marshall, Catherine. *Adventures in Prayer.* Old Tappan, NJ:
Fleming H. Revell Company, 1975. Teaches eight types
of prayer, ending each chapter with a prayer that
readers can apply to their own lives.

Parker, William R., and St. Johns, Elaine. *Prayer Can Change Your Life.* Englewood Cliffs, NJ: Prentice-Hall, Inc., 1957. A realistic approach to the dynamics of personal prayer.

Peale, Norman Vincent. *The Power of Positive Thinking.* New York: Prentice-Hall, 1952. Using personal experience examples, Peale leads the reader toward more positive, effective ways of praying.

Peale, Norman Vincent. *Positive Imaging.* New York: Ballantine Books, 1982. Teaches the principle of visualization as an effective and practical form of prayer.

Rinker, Rosalind. *Praying Together.* Grand Rapids, MI: Zondervan, 1968. This is helpful for those who are uncomfortable when asked to pray aloud. It is also useful for prayer groups.

Praying with the Bible

Helleberg, Marilyn Morgan. *Where Soul and Spirit Meet: Praying with the Bible.* Nashville, TN: Abingdon Press, 1986. Explains how to meet God Himself in the pages of the Bible and offers themes for thirty weeks of Scriptural prayer.

Mischke, Bernard, and Mischke, Fritz. *Pray Today's Gospel.* New York: Alba House, 1980. Thoughts and reflections on the gospel message for each day.

Rosage, David E. *Listen to Him.* Ann Arbor: Servant Books, 1981. An easy-to-use program of Scripture reading and meditation with themes and readings for fifty-two weeks.

Books on Creativity

Bach, Marcus. *The World of Serendipity.* Marina del Rey, CA: DeVorss & Co., 1970. With charm and wit, the author encourages readers to develop creativity by learning to expect the unexpected.

Fox, Emmet. *Find and Use Your Inner Power.* New York: Harper & Bros., 1941. Fox believes that the will of God for humans is freedom, health, and harmony, and he offers principles for making these qualities a reality in everyday life.

Garfield, Patricia. *Creative Dreaming.* New York: Simon & Schuster, 1974. A guide for increasing creativity through working with one's dreams.

Ghiselin, Brewster, editor. *The Creative Process.* New York: The New American Library, 1952. A collection of comments on creativity from thirty-eight brilliant men and women.

Goldberg, Philip. *The Intuitive Edge.* Los Angeles: Jeremy P. Tarcher, Inc., 1983. Goldberg teaches the reader what intuition is and how to cultivate it.

Harman, Willis, and Rheingold, Howard. *Higher Creativity.* Los Angeles: Jeremy P. Tarcher, Inc., 1984. The authors examine ways that all people can use to develop their inborn creativity.

Karagulla, Shafica. *Breakthrough to Creativity.* Los Angeles: DeVorss & Co., 1972. This book places a special emphasis on the spiritual elements in creativity.

LeBoeuf, Michael. *Imagineering.* New York: McGraw-Hill, 1980. Offers specific, directed ways to increase creative ability.

May, Rollo. *The Courage to Create.* New York: W. W. Norton & Co., Inc., 1975. Dr. May explores the power of creativity as the highest and most healthy human trait.

O'Connor, Elizabeth. *Eighth Day of Creation.* Waco, Texas: Word Books, 1971. The author suggests ways of discovering one's God-given gifts and offers selected excerpts from various writers, intended to stimulate creative thinking.

Zdenek, Marilee. *The Right-Brain Experience.* New York: McGraw-Hill, 1983. Includes interviews with well-known creative people, as well as a six-day personal program for learning to draw on the creative right hemisphere of the brain.

CHRISTIAN HERALD
People Making A Difference

Christian Herald is a family of dedicated, Christ-centered ministries that reaches out to deprived children in need, and to homeless men who are lost in alcoholism and drug addiction. Christian Herald also offers the finest in family and evangelical literature through its book clubs and publishes a popular, dynamic magazine for today's Christians.

Our Ministries

Family Bookshelf and **Christian Bookshelf** provide a wide selection of inspirational reading and Christian literature written by best-selling authors. All books are recommended by an Advisory Board of distinguished writers and editors.

Christian Herald magazine is contemporary, a dynamic publication that addresses the vital concerns of today's Christian. Each monthly issue contains a sharing of true personal stories written by people who have found in Christ the strength to make a difference in the world around them.

Christian Herald Children. The door of God's grace opens wide to give impoverished youngsters a breath of fresh air, away from the evils of the streets. Every summer, hundreds of youngsters are welcomed at the Christian Herald Mont Lawn Camp located in the Poconos at Bushkill, Pennsylvania. Year-round assistance is also provided, including teen programs, tutoring in reading and writing, family counseling, career guidance and college scholarship programs.

The Bowery Mission. Located in New York City, the Bowery Mission offers hope and Gospel strength to the downtrodden and homeless. Here, the men of Skid Row are fed, clothed, ministered to. Many voluntarily enter a 6-month discipleship program of spiritual guidance, nutrition therapy and Bible study.

Our Father's House. Located in rural Pennsylvania, Our Father's House is a discipleship and job training center. Alcoholics and drug addicts are given an opportunity to recover, away from the temptations of city streets.

Christian Herald ministries, founded in 1878, are supported by the voluntary contributions of individuals and by legacies and bequests. Contributions are tax deductible. Checks should be made out to Christian Herald Children, The Bowery Mission, or to Christian Herald Association.

Administrative Office: 40 Overlook Drive, Chappaqua, New York 10514
Telephone: (914) 769-9000

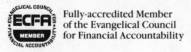

Fully-accredited Member
of the Evangelical Council
for Financial Accountability